Heart-Healthy Cookbook:

200+ Low-Fat, Low-Sodium Recipes to Lower Cholesterol, Manage Blood Pressure, and Keep Your Diet Delicious, Nourishing, and Balanced

Eden Hansen

© **2025 Eden Hansen. All rights reserved.**

This book may not be copied, stored in a retrieval system, or transmitted in any way, whether electronic, mechanical, photocopying, recording, or otherwise, without prior written permission from the publisher, except for brief excerpts used in scholarly works or reviews.

Disclaimer

This publication should only be used for educational and informational purposes; it should not be used as a substitute for expert medical advice, diagnosis, or care. Although the recipes, dietary advice, and nutritional data offered are intended to promote heart health in general, they might not be appropriate for all people.

Before adopting any dietary or lifestyle changes, always get advice from a certified healthcare provider, particularly if you have a medical condition, are on medication, or have special dietary requirements. The publisher and the author disclaim all responsibility for any negative consequences arising from using any content provided. The reader uses all information at their own risk and judgment.

Your path to improved heart health is unique; always make decisions based on your body's needs and seek advice from qualified experts as needed.

TABLE OF CONTENTS

INTRODUCTION 8

BREAKFAST 10
- *OATMEAL WITH BERRIES AND FLAXSEEDS* 11
- *AVOCADO TOAST WITH WHOLE-GRAIN BREAD* 11
- *CHIA SEED PUDDING WITH ALMOND MILK* 12
- *SCRAMBLED EGG WHITES WITH SPINACH AND FETA* 12
- *BLUEBERRY QUINOA BREAKFAST BOWL* 13
- *WHOLE-GRAIN PANCAKES WITH GREEK YOGURT* 13
- *APPLE CINNAMON OVERNIGHT OATS* 14
- *BANANA WALNUT MUFFINS (LOW-SUGAR)* 14
- *SMOKED SALMON AND AVOCADO ENGLISH MUFFIN* 15
- *TOFU SCRAMBLE WITH VEGETABLES* 15
- *GREEN SMOOTHIE WITH KALE AND PINEAPPLE* 16
- *ALMOND BUTTER AND BANANA OATMEAL* 16
- *HEART-HEALTHY GRANOLA WITH NUTS AND SEEDS* 17
- *COTTAGE CHEESE WITH BERRIES AND CHIA* 17
- *SWEET POTATO AND BLACK BEAN BREAKFAST BURRITO* 18
- *MEDITERRANEAN-STYLE EGG MUFFINS* 18
- *BAKED OATMEAL WITH PEACHES AND PECANS* 19
- *WHOLE-GRAIN WAFFLES WITH FRESH BERRIES* 19
- *WARM QUINOA PORRIDGE WITH ALMONDS* 20
- *GREEK YOGURT PARFAIT WITH MIXED BERRIES* 20
- *SPINACH AND TOMATO FRITTATA* 21
- *MATCHA CHIA PUDDING* 21
- *HIGH-FIBER BRAN MUFFINS* 22
- *PEANUT BUTTER AND APPLE SLICES ON RYE TOAST* 22
- *BAKED AVOCADO EGG CUPS* 23
- *ZUCCHINI AND CARROT BREAKFAST LOAF* 23

SNACKS AND APPETIZERS 24
- *ROASTED CHICKPEAS WITH PAPRIKA* 25
- *CUCUMBER AND HUMMUS BITES* 25
- *AVOCADO DEVILED EGGS* 26
- *BAKED KALE CHIPS WITH GARLIC* 26
- *SWEET POTATO HUMMUS WITH VEGGIE STICKS* 27
- *TOMATO AND BASIL BRUSCHETTA ON WHOLE-GRAIN TOAST* 27
- *BAKED ZUCCHINI FRIES* 28
- *ROASTED RED PEPPER AND WALNUT DIP* 28
- *GREEK YOGURT RANCH DIP WITH CARROTS* 29
- *EDAMAME WITH SEA SALT AND LEMON* 29
- *MINI CAPRESE SKEWERS WITH BALSAMIC GLAZE* 30
- *SPICY ROASTED ALMONDS* 30
- *MANGO SALSA WITH BAKED TORTILLA CHIPS* 31
- *WHOLE-WHEAT PITA CHIPS WITH GUACAMOLE* 31
- *LENTIL AND SPINACH PATTIES* 32
- *HEART-HEALTHY TRAIL MIX WITH DARK CHOCOLATE* 32
- *STUFFED MUSHROOMS WITH RICOTTA AND HERBS* 33

AIR-FRIED CAULIFLOWER BUFFALO BITES 33
SMOKED SALMON AND CUCUMBER ROLLS 34
BALSAMIC ROASTED BRUSSELS SPROUTS 34
ALMOND BUTTER AND DATE ENERGY BITES 35
MASHED AVOCADO ON RYE CRACKERS 35
GARLIC AND HERB ROASTED CASHEWS 36
GRILLED EGGPLANT WITH LEMON AND OLIVE OIL 36
SPICED PUMPKIN SEEDS 37
GREEK YOGURT WITH HONEY AND WALNUTS 37

SALADS AND SIDES 38

QUINOA AND KALE SALAD WITH LEMON DRESSING 39
MEDITERRANEAN CHICKPEA SALAD 39
ROASTED BEET AND ARUGULA SALAD 40
LENTIL AND SPINACH SALAD WITH BALSAMIC VINAIGRETTE 40
AVOCADO AND TOMATO SALAD WITH OLIVE OIL 41
RAINBOW SLAW WITH CITRUS DRESSING 41
GRILLED ASPARAGUS WITH LEMON ZEST 42
SWEET POTATO AND BLACK BEAN SALAD 42
CUCUMBER, TOMATO, AND FETA SALAD 43
WARM FARRO SALAD WITH ROASTED VEGETABLES 43
GARLIC AND HERB ROASTED CAULIFLOWER 44
BROCCOLI AND ALMOND SALAD WITH YOGURT DRESSING 44
CARROT AND GINGER SLAW 45
WILD RICE AND CRANBERRY PILAF 45
SPINACH AND STRAWBERRY SALAD WITH WALNUTS 46
ROASTED BRUSSELS SPROUTS WITH POMEGRANATE SEEDS 46
MARINATED ARTICHOKES AND OLIVES 47
GRILLED ZUCCHINI AND RED PEPPERS 47
WATERMELON AND FETA SALAD WITH MINT 48
TOMATO AND WHITE BEAN SALAD 48
CABBAGE AND APPLE SLAW 49
WHOLE-WHEAT COUSCOUS WITH NUTS AND RAISINS 49
GREEN BEAN SALAD WITH ALMONDS 50
BALSAMIC MUSHROOMS WITH GARLIC 50
SWEET CORN AND AVOCADO SALAD 51
BUTTERNUT SQUASH AND QUINOA SIDE 51

SOUPS AND STEWS 52

LENTIL AND SPINACH SOUP 53
TOMATO AND WHITE BEAN SOUP 53
BUTTERNUT SQUASH AND GINGER SOUP 54
HEARTY VEGETABLE BARLEY SOUP 54
MEDITERRANEAN MINESTRONE 55
CAULIFLOWER AND LEEK SOUP 55
BLACK BEAN AND SWEET POTATO STEW 56
CREAMY CARROT AND TURMERIC SOUP 56
CHICKPEA AND KALE STEW 57
MUSHROOM AND WILD RICE SOUP 57

SPICED PUMPKIN SOUP 58
LEMON AND DILL CHICKEN SOUP 58
QUINOA AND RED LENTIL SOUP 59
ROASTED GARLIC AND TOMATO SOUP 59
SPICY MOROCCAN CHICKPEA SOUP 60
GREEN PEA AND MINT SOUP.. 60
MISO SOUP WITH TOFU AND SEAWEED 61
BROCCOLI AND ALMOND SOUP 61
SLOW-COOKED TOMATO BASIL SOUP 62
ZUCCHINI AND SPINACH SOUP 62
RED CABBAGE AND APPLE SOUP 63
GINGERED CARROT AND COCONUT SOUP 63
SWEET CORN AND ROASTED RED PEPPER SOUP 64
CABBAGE AND LENTIL SOUP... 64
CHILLED CUCUMBER AND AVOCADO SOUP 65
MUSHROOM AND ONION SOUP 65

POULTRY 66

LEMON GARLIC CHICKEN BREAST... 67
BALSAMIC GRILLED CHICKEN WITH VEGGIES 67
HERB-ROASTED CHICKEN THIGHS 68
SPICY TANDOORI CHICKEN 68
CHICKEN AND QUINOA STIR-FRY 69
MEDITERRANEAN CHICKEN WRAP 69
GRILLED CHICKEN WITH MANGO SALSA 70
SPINACH AND FETA STUFFED CHICKEN 70
HONEY MUSTARD GLAZED CHICKEN 71
GARLIC-LIME CHICKEN SKEWERS... 71
SLOW COOKER CHICKEN AND VEGETABLES 72
TURMERIC AND GINGER CHICKEN SOUP.. 72
BAKED LEMON-HERB CHICKEN TENDERS 73
GREEK CHICKEN WITH OLIVES 73
COCONUT LIME CHICKEN 74
CHICKEN AND CHICKPEA STEW 74
HONEY GARLIC CHICKEN WITH BROCCOLI 75
SMOKED PAPRIKA ROASTED CHICKEN.. 75
CHICKEN WITH ROASTED RED PEPPERS 76
CRANBERRY WALNUT CHICKEN SALAD 76
LEMON-DIJON GRILLED CHICKEN 77
CHICKEN AND ZUCCHINI SKILLET 77
AVOCADO CHICKEN SALAD WRAP... 78
ORANGE GINGER GLAZED CHICKEN 78
SPICY PEANUT CHICKEN STIR-FRY 79
CUMIN AND CORIANDER CHICKEN 79

SEAFOOD 80

GRILLED SALMON WITH LEMON AND DILL 81
BAKED COD WITH GARLIC AND TOMATOES... 81
BLACKENED TILAPIA WITH LIME.. 82

- GINGER SOY GLAZED SALMON 82
- SHRIMP AND AVOCADO SALAD 83
- MISO-GLAZED HALIBUT 83
- GARLIC-LEMON SHRIMP SKEWERS 84
- SEARED TUNA WITH SESAME CRUST 84
- SCALLOPS WITH CITRUS DRESSING 85
- HERB-CRUSTED BAKED FISH 85
- MEDITERRANEAN SHRIMP STIR-FRY 86
- TERIYAKI SALMON WITH BROWN RICE 86
- POACHED COD IN TOMATO BROTH 87
- GRILLED MAHI-MAHI WITH PINEAPPLE SALSA 87
- DIJON MUSTARD ROASTED TROUT 88
- SPICY GARLIC SHRIMP 88
- ALMOND-CRUSTED TILAPIA 89
- SMOKED SALMON AND CUCUMBER ROLLS 89
- TUNA AND WHITE BEAN SALAD 90
- LEMON HERB BAKED SCALLOPS 90
- STEAMED MUSSELS IN WHITE WINE 91
- SARDINE AND TOMATO BRUSCHETTA 91
- OVEN-ROASTED HALIBUT WITH ROSEMARY 92
- BAKED TROUT WITH ALMONDS 92
- CILANTRO LIME SHRIMP BOWL 93
- MEDITERRANEAN GRILLED OCTOPUS 93

VEGETARIAN MEALS 94
- LENTIL AND SWEET POTATO CURRY 95
- QUINOA AND BLACK BEAN TACOS 95
- CHICKPEA AND SPINACH STIR-FRY 96
- STUFFED BELL PEPPERS WITH BROWN RICE 96
- BAKED EGGPLANT PARMESAN 97
- SPAGHETTI SQUASH WITH TOMATO BASIL SAUCE 97
- CAULIFLOWER AND CHICKPEA MASALA 98
- MEDITERRANEAN LENTIL AND FETA WRAP 98
- SWEET POTATO AND BLACK BEAN ENCHILADAS 99
- ROASTED VEGETABLE AND HUMMUS WRAP 99
- ZUCCHINI NOODLES WITH AVOCADO PESTO 100
- HEARTY THREE-BEAN CHILI 100
- MUSHROOM AND SPINACH QUICHE 101
- BROCCOLI AND TOFU STIR-FRY 101
- ROASTED BUTTERNUT SQUASH AND KALE BOWL 102
- CHICKPEA AND QUINOA STUFFED TOMATOES 102
- BAKED FALAFEL WITH TAHINI DRESSING 103
- GREEK-STYLE STUFFED PEPPERS 103
- SPICED LENTIL AND CARROT PATTIES 104
- PORTOBELLO MUSHROOM AND AVOCADO BURGER 104
- VEGAN SHEPHERD'S PIE WITH MASHED CAULIFLOWER 105
- MOROCCAN CHICKPEA AND COUSCOUS BOWL 105
- BLACK BEAN AND CORN-STUFFED SWEET POTATOES 106
- ROASTED BRUSSELS SPROUTS WITH QUINOA AND CRANBERRIES 106

- RATATOUILLE WITH HERBED POLENTA 107
- ASIAN-INSPIRED SESAME TOFU WITH BOK CHOY 107

DESSERTS 108

- AVOCADO CHOCOLATE MOUSSE 109
- OATMEAL BANANA COOKIES 109
- ALMOND BUTTER BROWNIES 110
- CHIA SEED BERRY PUDDING 110
- DARK CHOCOLATE AND WALNUT BARK 111
- APPLE CINNAMON BAKED OATMEAL 111
- RASPBERRY CHIA JAM BARS 112
- BLUEBERRY ALMOND CRISP 112
- PUMPKIN SPICE ENERGY BITES 113
- COCONUT AND DATE BLISS BALLS 113
- MANGO AND COCONUT CHIA PARFAIT 114
- CHOCOLATE-DIPPED STRAWBERRIES WITH NUTS 114
- BAKED PEACHES WITH HONEY AND CINNAMON 115
- VEGAN PEANUT BUTTER CUPS 115
- LEMON POPPY SEED MUFFINS 116
- SPICED APPLE COMPOTE WITH GREEK YOGURT 116
- BLACK BEAN AND DARK CHOCOLATE FUDGE 117
- CARROT CAKE ENERGY BITES 117
- VANILLA CHIA PUDDING WITH BERRIES 118
- ROASTED PEARS WITH ALMOND BUTTER DRIZZLE 118
- WHOLE-WHEAT BANANA BREAD 119
- MATCHA GREEN TEA AND COCONUT POPSICLES 119
- STRAWBERRY AND OAT CRUMBLE BARS 120
- SWEET POTATO CHOCOLATE CHIP COOKIES 120
- CINNAMON ROASTED ALMONDS 121
- NO-BAKE CASHEW AND DATE BARS 121

Introduction

Welcome to your heart-healthy diet cookbook, a practical and informative guide to cooking meals that promote cardiovascular health without sacrificing flavor or satisfaction. In today's world, where processed foods and fast meals are readily available, it's easy to lose sight of how much the food we eat directly impacts the health of our heart. This cookbook is here to help you take back control in the most nourishing and enjoyable way possible — right from your kitchen.

A heart-healthy diet isn't a short-term fix or a restrictive fad. It's a long-term, sustainable approach to eating that supports the health of your entire cardiovascular system. This means protecting your arteries, lowering your blood pressure, balancing cholesterol levels, and reducing inflammation, all of which can help prevent serious conditions like heart attacks, strokes, and heart failure. The foundation of this diet lies in real, whole foods prepared in simple ways that preserve their nutritional value while enhancing their taste.

At the center of the heart-healthy diet are ingredients that are naturally rich in fiber, antioxidants, vitamins, and healthy fats. Fresh fruits and vegetables provide vital nutrients and are especially important for their high content of heart-protective compounds like potassium and polyphenols. Whole grains such as oats, quinoa, brown rice, and whole-wheat products offer complex carbohydrates that support steady energy levels and help control blood sugar. Lean proteins like fish — particularly fatty fish such as salmon and mackerel — legumes, tofu, and skinless poultry help build and repair tissues without the excess saturated fat found in red meats.

Healthy fats are essential for heart function and overall well-being. Rather than avoiding fat altogether, this diet encourages the use of unsaturated fats from sources like olive oil, avocados, nuts, and seeds. These fats have been shown to improve cholesterol profiles and support the health of blood vessels. In contrast, saturated fats — commonly found in butter, cream, fatty cuts of meat, and full-fat dairy — should be consumed sparingly. Trans fats, often found in commercial baked goods, margarine, and processed snacks should be avoided altogether, as they have a direct negative effect on cholesterol levels.

Sodium and added sugars are two additional elements that can undermine heart health when consumed in excess. A heart-healthy eating plan prioritizes fresh and minimally processed foods to help naturally reduce sodium intake. Herbs, spices, citrus, and vinegar are all encouraged as flavorful alternatives to salt. Similarly, desserts, sweetened beverages, and packaged snacks with added sugars are replaced with naturally sweet options like fruit or small amounts of dark chocolate.

This cookbook is designed for anyone who wants to take better care of their heart through diet, whether you've been advised by a healthcare provider to make changes, or you're simply looking to maintain a healthy lifestyle and prevent problems down the road. It's especially valuable for people with high blood pressure, elevated cholesterol, a family history of heart disease, or metabolic concerns like prediabetes or type 2 diabetes. However, these meals aren't just good for you — they're full of flavor, variety, and joy, making them a great fit for the entire family.

The cooking methods featured throughout this book are just as important as the ingredients themselves. Techniques such as baking, grilling, steaming, roasting, and sautéing with small amounts of healthy oil help retain nutrients while keeping saturated fat content low. You'll find that these approaches not only preserve the flavor and texture of your ingredients but also promote a lighter, cleaner way of eating that still feels satisfying.

What makes this lifestyle sustainable is its flexibility and realism. You don't have to follow it perfectly every day to see the benefits. Progress comes from consistent choices over time — like replacing white bread with whole grain, enjoying a fresh salad instead of chips, or preparing a homemade meal instead of ordering fast food. Every small decision adds up to better heart health, improved energy, and a stronger foundation for lifelong wellness.

As you explore the recipes in this book, you'll find that eating for your heart doesn't mean sacrificing comfort, pleasure, or convenience. On the contrary, it's a chance to rediscover the beauty of cooking with intention — choosing ingredients with care, experimenting with flavors, and enjoying meals that are good for your body and soul.

Thank you for choosing to prioritize your health through the power of food. May your time in the kitchen be full of discovery, your meals be satisfying and nourishing, and your heart grow stronger with every bite.

Wishing you warmth, wellness, and joy on your cooking journey.

Breakfast

OATMEAL WITH BERRIES AND FLAXSEEDS

Servings 2 | Prep: 5 min | Cook: 10 min

Start your day with this heart-healthy oatmeal, packed with antioxidants from berries and omega-3s from flaxseeds. It's a delicious and nutritious way to fuel your morning.

Equipment

Saucepan, Measuring Cups, Spoon

Ingredients

- 80 g Rolled Oats
- 500 ml Water
- 100 g Mixed Berries (such as blueberries, strawberries, raspberries)
- 15 g Ground Flaxseeds
- 10 ml Honey (optional)
- 1 g Cinnamon (optional)

Directions

1. In a saucepan, bring the water to a boil.
2. Add the rolled oats and reduce the heat to a simmer. Cook for about 5 minutes, stirring occasionally.
3. Stir in the mixed berries and cook for an additional 2-3 minutes until the berries are warm and the oatmeal is creamy.
4. Remove from heat and stir in the ground flaxseeds.
5. If desired, add honey and a sprinkle of cinnamon for extra flavor.
6. Serve hot and enjoy your heart-healthy breakfast.

Nutritional Information

Calories: 250, Protein: 7g, Carbohydrates: 45g, Fat: 6g, Fiber: 8g, Cholesterol: 0 mg, Salt: 5 mg, Potassium: 250 mg

AVOCADO TOAST WITH WHOLE-GRAIN BREAD

Servings 2 | Prep: 10 min | Cook: 0 min

This simple yet delicious avocado toast is a perfect heart-healthy breakfast option. Packed with healthy fats, fiber, and essential nutrients, it's a great way to start your day.

Equipment

Toaster, Knife, Fork

Ingredients

- 2 slices whole-grain bread (approximately 60g per slice)
- 1 ripe avocado (about 150g)
- 10 ml fresh lemon juice
- 5g extra virgin olive oil
- 2g salt
- 2g black pepper
- Optional toppings: 10g cherry tomatoes, 5g radish slices, 5g fresh herbs (such as cilantro or parsley)

Directions

1. Toast the whole-grain bread slices to your desired level of crispiness.
2. While the bread is toasting, cut the avocado in half, remove the pit, and scoop the flesh into a bowl.
3. Add the lemon juice, olive oil, salt, and pepper to the avocado. Mash with a fork until smooth but still slightly chunky.
4. Spread the avocado mixture evenly over the toasted bread slices.
5. Top with optional toppings like cherry tomatoes, radish slices, or fresh herbs for added flavor and nutrition.

Nutritional Information

Calories: 250, Protein: 5g, Carbohydrates: 30g, Fat: 15g, Fiber: 8g, Cholesterol: 0mg, Salt: 300mg, Potassium: 500mg

CHIA SEED PUDDING WITH ALMOND MILK

Servings 2 | Prep: 5 min | Cook: 0 min

This creamy chia seed pudding is a heart-healthy breakfast option, packed with omega-3 fatty acids, fiber, and antioxidants. It's a simple, make-ahead meal that will keep you energized throughout the morning.

Equipment

Mixing Bowl, Whisk, Measuring Cups

Ingredients

- 60 g Chia Seeds
- 500 ml Unsweetened Almond Milk
- 15 ml Maple Syrup
- 5 ml Vanilla Extract
- 100 g Fresh Berries (e.g., blueberries, strawberries)

Directions

1. In a mixing bowl, combine chia seeds, almond milk, maple syrup, and vanilla extract.
2. Whisk the mixture thoroughly to ensure the chia seeds are evenly distributed.
3. Cover the bowl and refrigerate for at least 4 hours or overnight to allow the pudding to thicken.
4. Before serving, stir the pudding to break up any clumps.
5. Top with fresh berries and enjoy.

Nutritional Information

Calories: 250, Protein: 6g, Carbohydrates: 30g, Fat: 12g, Fiber: 10g, Cholesterol: 0 mg, Salt: 50 mg, Potassium: 300 mg

SCRAMBLED EGG WHITES WITH SPINACH AND FETA

Servings 2 | Prep: 5 min | Cook: 10 min

A light and nutritious breakfast option, this dish combines fluffy egg whites with the vibrant flavors of spinach and creamy feta cheese, perfect for a heart-healthy start to your day.

Equipment

Non-stick skillet, Whisk, Spatula

Ingredients

- 240 ml egg whites (approximately 8 egg whites)
- 100 g fresh spinach, chopped
- 50 g feta cheese, crumbled
- 10 ml olive oil
- 1 g black pepper
- 1 g salt (optional)

Directions

1. Heat the olive oil in a non-stick skillet over medium heat.
2. Add the chopped spinach to the skillet and sauté until wilted, about 2-3 minutes.
3. In a bowl, whisk the egg whites with black pepper and salt (if using) until frothy.
4. Pour the egg whites into the skillet with the spinach, stirring gently with a spatula.
5. Cook until the egg whites are set but still soft, about 3-4 minutes.
6. Sprinkle the crumbled feta cheese over the eggs and fold gently to combine.
7. Serve immediately, garnished with additional black pepper if desired.

Nutritional Information

Calories: 150, Protein: 20g, Carbohydrates: 4g, Fat: 7g, Fiber: 1g, Cholesterol: 15 mg, Salt: 350 mg, Potassium: 500 mg

BLUEBERRY QUINOA BREAKFAST BOWL

Servings 2 | Prep: 5 min | Cook: 15 min

This hearty and nutritious breakfast bowl combines the protein-rich goodness of quinoa with the antioxidant power of blueberries, making it a perfect start to your day.

Equipment

Medium Saucepan, Measuring Cups, Spoon

Ingredients

- 100 g quinoa
- 250 ml water
- 150 g fresh blueberries
- 100 ml almond milk
- 10 g honey
- 5 g chia seeds
- 1 g cinnamon powder

Directions

1. Rinse the quinoa under cold water.
2. In a medium saucepan, combine quinoa and water. Bring to a boil, then reduce heat and simmer for 15 minutes or until water is absorbed.
3. Stir in almond milk, honey, and cinnamon. Cook for an additional 2 minutes.
4. Remove from heat and gently fold in the blueberries and chia seeds.
5. Divide into bowls and serve warm.

Nutritional Information

Calories: 250, Protein: 6g, Carbohydrates: 45g, Fat: 4g, Fiber: 6g, Cholesterol: 0 mg, Salt: 10 mg, Potassium: 200 mg

WHOLE-GRAIN PANCAKES WITH GREEK YOGURT

Servings 4 | Prep: 10 min | Cook: 15 min

These whole-grain pancakes are a heart-healthy breakfast option, combining the nutty flavor of whole grains with the creamy tang of Greek yogurt. Perfect for a nutritious start to your day.

Equipment

Mixing Bowl, Whisk, Non-stick Skillet

Ingredients

- 150 g whole wheat flour
- 10 g baking powder
- 2 g salt
- 200 ml skim milk
- 1 large egg
- 15 ml olive oil
- 100 g Greek yogurt
- 15 ml honey
- 5 ml vanilla extract

Directions

1. In a mixing bowl, combine the whole wheat flour, baking powder, and salt.
2. In a separate bowl, whisk together the skim milk, egg, olive oil, Greek yogurt, honey, and vanilla extract until smooth.
3. Gradually add the wet ingredients to the dry ingredients, stirring until just combined.
4. Heat a non-stick skillet over medium heat and lightly grease with a small amount of olive oil.
5. Pour 60 ml of batter onto the skillet for each pancake. Cook until bubbles form on the surface, then flip and cook until golden brown.
6. Serve warm, topped with a dollop of Greek yogurt and a drizzle of honey, if desired.

Nutritional Information

Calories: 210, Protein: 8g, Carbohydrates: 30g, Fat: 6g, Fiber: 4g, Cholesterol: 35 mg, Salt: 250 mg, Potassium: 180 mg

APPLE CINNAMON OVERNIGHT OATS

Servings 2 | Prep: 10 min | Cook: 0 min

Wake up to a heart-healthy breakfast with these Apple Cinnamon Overnight Oats. This easy, no-cook recipe is perfect for busy mornings, offering a delicious blend of creamy oats, sweet apples, and warming cinnamon.

Equipment

Mixing Bowl, Measuring Cups, Spoon, Jar or Container with Lid

Ingredients

- 100 g Rolled Oats
- 250 ml Unsweetened Almond Milk
- 1 Medium Apple (about 150 g), diced
- 10 g Chia Seeds
- 5 g Ground Cinnamon
- 15 ml Honey (optional)
- 5 g Chopped Walnuts (optional)

Directions

1. In a mixing bowl, combine the rolled oats, almond milk, chia seeds, and ground cinnamon. Stir well.
2. Add the diced apple to the mixture and stir until evenly distributed.
3. If desired, add honey for sweetness and mix thoroughly.
4. Transfer the mixture to a jar or container with a lid. Seal and refrigerate overnight.
5. In the morning, give the oats a good stir and top with chopped walnuts before serving.

Nutritional Information

Calories: 250, Protein: 6g, Carbohydrates: 45g, Fat: 6g, Fiber: 8g, Cholesterol: 0 mg, Salt: 50 mg, Potassium: 250 mg

BANANA WALNUT MUFFINS (LOW-SUGAR)

Servings 12 | Prep: 15 min | Cook: 20 min

These moist and flavorful muffins are a heart-healthy way to start your day, combining the natural sweetness of bananas with the crunch of walnuts.

Equipment

Mixing Bowl, Muffin Tin, Whisk

Ingredients

- 300 g ripe bananas (about 3 medium bananas)
- 60 ml olive oil
- 60 ml unsweetened applesauce
- 1 large egg
- 5 ml vanilla extract
- 200 g whole wheat flour
- 5 g baking soda
- 2 g salt
- 50 g chopped walnuts

Directions

1. Preheat the oven to 180°C and line a muffin tin with paper liners.
2. In a mixing bowl, mash the bananas until smooth.
3. Add olive oil, applesauce, egg, and vanilla extract to the bananas and whisk until well combined.
4. In a separate bowl, mix the whole wheat flour, baking soda, and salt.
5. Gradually add the dry ingredients to the wet mixture, stirring until just combined.
6. Fold in the chopped walnuts.
7. Divide the batter evenly among the muffin cups and bake for 18-20 minutes, or until a toothpick inserted into the center comes out clean.

Nutritional Information

Calories: 150, Protein: 3g, Carbohydrates: 20g, Fat: 7g, Fiber: 3g, Cholesterol: 10 mg, Salt: 150 mg, Potassium: 200 mg

SMOKED SALMON AND AVOCADO ENGLISH MUFFIN

Servings 2 | Prep: 10 min | Cook: 5 min

A delightful and nutritious start to your day, this smoked salmon and avocado English muffin combines creamy avocado with the rich flavor of smoked salmon, all atop a toasted whole grain muffin.

Equipment

Toaster, Knife, Cutting Board

Ingredients

- 2 whole grain English muffins (approximately 120 g)
- 100 g smoked salmon
- 1 ripe avocado (approximately 150 g)
- 10 ml lemon juice
- 10 g fresh dill, chopped
- 5 g capers, rinsed
- Salt and pepper to taste

Directions

1. Slice the English muffins in half and toast them until golden brown.
2. While the muffins are toasting, halve the avocado, remove the pit, and scoop the flesh into a bowl. Mash with a fork and mix in the lemon juice, salt, and pepper.
3. Spread the mashed avocado evenly over each toasted muffin half.
4. Layer the smoked salmon slices on top of the avocado.
5. Garnish with fresh dill and capers before serving.

Nutritional Information

Calories: 320, Protein: 15g, Carbohydrates: 28g, Fat: 18g, Fiber: 7g, Cholesterol: 25 mg, Salt: 600 mg, Potassium: 600 mg

TOFU SCRAMBLE WITH VEGETABLES

Servings 4 | Prep: 10 min | Cook: 15 min

This vibrant tofu scramble is a delightful and nutritious way to start your day, packed with colorful vegetables and seasoned to perfection.

Equipment

Non-stick skillet, Spatula, Mixing bowl

Ingredients

- 400 g firm tofu, drained and crumbled
- 15 ml olive oil
- 100 g bell peppers, diced
- 100 g spinach, chopped
- 50 g onion, finely chopped
- 2 cloves garlic, minced
- 5 g turmeric powder
- 5 g nutritional yeast
- Salt and pepper to taste

Directions

1. Heat olive oil in a non-stick skillet over medium heat.
2. Add onions and garlic, sauté until onions are translucent.
3. Stir in bell peppers and cook for 3 minutes.
4. Add crumbled tofu, turmeric, and nutritional yeast, mixing well.
5. Fold in spinach and cook until wilted. Season with salt and pepper.
6. Serve hot, garnished with fresh herbs if desired.

Nutritional Information

Calories: 180, Protein: 14g, Carbohydrates: 10g, Fat: 10g, Fiber: 4g, Cholesterol: 0 mg, Salt: 150 mg, Potassium: 450 mg

GREEN SMOOTHIE WITH KALE AND PINEAPPLE

Servings 2 | Prep: 10 min | Cook: 0 min

This vibrant green smoothie combines the earthy goodness of kale with the tropical sweetness of pineapple, creating a refreshing and heart-healthy start to your day.

Equipment

Blender, Measuring Cups, Knife

Ingredients

- 100 g Kale, washed and chopped
- 150 g Pineapple, peeled and diced
- 1 Banana, medium-sized
- 250 ml Unsweetened Almond Milk
- 10 g Chia Seeds
- 5 ml Fresh Lemon Juice

Directions

1. Add the kale, pineapple, and banana to the blender.
2. Pour in the almond milk and add the chia seeds.
3. Squeeze in the fresh lemon juice for a hint of brightness.
4. Blend on high speed until smooth and creamy.
5. Pour into glasses and serve immediately.

Nutritional Information

Calories: 180, Protein: 4g, Carbohydrates: 38g, Fat: 3g, Fiber: 6g, Cholesterol: 0 mg, Salt: 50 mg, Potassium: 500 mg

ALMOND BUTTER AND BANANA OATMEAL

Servings 2 | Prep: 5 min | Cook: 10 min

This creamy and satisfying oatmeal combines the nutty richness of almond butter with the natural sweetness of bananas, making it a perfect heart-healthy start to your day.

Equipment

Saucepan, Stirring Spoon, Measuring Cups

Ingredients

- 80 g rolled oats
- 500 ml water
- 1 medium banana, sliced
- 30 g almond butter
- 10 g chia seeds
- 5 ml honey (optional)
- A pinch of cinnamon

Directions

1. In a saucepan, bring the water to a boil.
2. Add the rolled oats and reduce the heat to a simmer. Cook for about 5 minutes, stirring occasionally.
3. Stir in the sliced banana, almond butter, and chia seeds. Cook for an additional 3-5 minutes until the oatmeal reaches your desired consistency.
4. Remove from heat and stir in honey and cinnamon, if using.
5. Divide the oatmeal into bowls and serve warm.

Nutritional Information

Calories: 320, Protein: 8g, Carbohydrates: 50g, Fat: 12g, Fiber: 8g, Cholesterol: 0 mg, Salt: 5 mg, Potassium: 450 mg

HEART-HEALTHY GRANOLA WITH NUTS AND SEEDS

Servings 8 | Prep: 10 min | Cook: 25 min

This heart-healthy granola is a delightful blend of oats, nuts, and seeds, offering a crunchy and nutritious start to your day. Perfect for breakfast or a snack, it's packed with fiber and healthy fats to support heart health.

Equipment

Baking Tray, Mixing Bowl, Oven

Ingredients

- 300 g Rolled Oats
- 100 g Almonds, chopped
- 50 g Walnuts, chopped
- 50 g Sunflower Seeds
- 50 g Pumpkin Seeds
- 60 ml Honey
- 30 ml Olive Oil
- 1 tsp Cinnamon
- 1/2 tsp Salt

Directions

1. Preheat the oven to 160°C (320°F).
2. In a mixing bowl, combine oats, almonds, walnuts, sunflower seeds, and pumpkin seeds.
3. In a small bowl, whisk together honey, olive oil, cinnamon, and salt.
4. Pour the honey mixture over the oat mixture and stir until evenly coated.
5. Spread the mixture onto a baking tray in an even layer.
6. Bake for 25 minutes, stirring halfway through, until golden brown.
7. Allow to cool completely before storing in an airtight container.

Nutritional Information

Calories: 250, Protein: 6g, Carbohydrates: 30g, Fat: 12g, Fiber: 4g, Cholesterol: 0 mg, Salt: 100 mg, Potassium: 200 mg

COTTAGE CHEESE WITH BERRIES AND CHIA

Servings 2 | Prep: 10 min | Cook: 0 min

This refreshing and nutritious breakfast combines creamy cottage cheese with the natural sweetness of berries and the health benefits of chia seeds, making it a perfect start to your day.

Equipment

Mixing Bowl, Spoon, Measuring Cups

Ingredients

- 200 g Cottage Cheese
- 100 g Mixed Berries (such as strawberries, blueberries, and raspberries)
- 15 g Chia Seeds
- 10 ml Honey (optional)
- 5 g Almonds, sliced (optional)

Directions

1. In a mixing bowl, combine the cottage cheese and chia seeds. Stir well to ensure the chia seeds are evenly distributed.
2. Gently fold in the mixed berries, being careful not to crush them.
3. If desired, drizzle honey over the mixture for added sweetness.
4. Sprinkle sliced almonds on top for a crunchy texture.
5. Serve immediately or refrigerate for up to 30 minutes to allow the chia seeds to soften slightly.

Nutritional Information

Calories: 180, Protein: 15g, Carbohydrates: 18g, Fat: 6g, Fiber: 5g, Cholesterol: 10 mg, Salt: 300 mg, Potassium: 250 mg

SWEET POTATO AND BLACK BEAN BREAKFAST BURRITO

Servings 4 | Prep: 15 min | Cook: 20 min

A hearty and nutritious breakfast burrito packed with the goodness of sweet potatoes and black beans, perfect for a heart-healthy start to your day.

Equipment

Skillet, Medium Saucepan, Mixing Bowl

Ingredients

- 400 g sweet potatoes, peeled and diced
- 200 g canned black beans, drained and rinsed
- 4 whole wheat tortillas
- 100 g red bell pepper, diced
- 50 g onion, finely chopped
- 2 cloves garlic, minced
- 10 ml olive oil
- 5 g ground cumin
- 5 g smoked paprika
- Salt and pepper to taste
- 30 g fresh cilantro, chopped

Directions

1. Boil the sweet potatoes in a medium saucepan until tender, about 10 minutes. Drain and set aside.
2. In a skillet, heat olive oil over medium heat. Add onion, garlic, and red bell pepper; sauté until softened.
3. Stir in the black beans, cooked sweet potatoes, cumin, smoked paprika, salt, and pepper. Cook for 5 minutes, stirring occasionally.
4. Warm the tortillas in a dry skillet or microwave.
5. Divide the sweet potato mixture among the tortillas, sprinkle with cilantro, and roll into burritos.

Nutritional Information

Calories: 320, Protein: 10g, Carbohydrates: 55g, Fat: 8g, Fiber: 12g, Cholesterol: 0 mg, Salt: 300 mg, Potassium: 700 mg

MEDITERRANEAN-STYLE EGG MUFFINS

Servings 6 | Prep: 10 min | Cook: 20 min

These Mediterranean-style egg muffins are a delightful and heart-healthy way to start your day. Packed with vegetables and herbs, they offer a burst of flavor in every bite.

Equipment

Muffin Tin, Mixing Bowl, Whisk

Ingredients

- 6 large eggs
- 100 g cherry tomatoes, halved
- 50 g spinach, chopped
- 50 g feta cheese, crumbled
- 30 ml low-fat milk
- 1 clove garlic, minced
- 5 g fresh basil, chopped
- 2 g salt
- 1 g black pepper

Directions

1. Preheat the oven to 180°C (350°F) and lightly grease a muffin tin.
2. In a mixing bowl, whisk together the eggs and milk until well combined.
3. Stir in the cherry tomatoes, spinach, feta cheese, garlic, basil, salt, and pepper.
4. Pour the egg mixture evenly into the prepared muffin tin, filling each cup about 3/4 full.
5. Bake in the preheated oven for 18-20 minutes, or until the egg muffins are set and lightly golden on top.
6. Allow to cool slightly before removing from the tin. Serve warm.

Nutritional Information

Calories: 110, Protein: 8g, Carbohydrates: 3g, Fat: 7g, Fiber: 1g, Cholesterol: 170 mg, Salt: 250 mg, Potassium: 200 mg

BAKED OATMEAL WITH PEACHES AND PECANS

Servings 6 | Prep: 10 min | Cook: 35 min

This heart-healthy baked oatmeal combines the natural sweetness of peaches with the crunch of pecans, offering a warm and comforting breakfast option that's both nutritious and delicious.

Equipment

Oven, Mixing Bowl, Baking Dish

Ingredients

- 200 g rolled oats
- 500 ml almond milk
- 2 large peaches, sliced
- 50 g pecans, chopped
- 50 g honey
- 1 tsp cinnamon
- 1 tsp baking powder
- 1/2 tsp salt
- 1 tsp vanilla extract

Directions

1. Preheat the oven to 180°C (350°F).
2. In a mixing bowl, combine oats, almond milk, honey, cinnamon, baking powder, salt, and vanilla extract. Mix well.
3. Fold in the sliced peaches and chopped pecans.
4. Pour the mixture into a baking dish and spread evenly.
5. Bake for 35 minutes or until the top is golden brown and the oatmeal is set.
6. Allow to cool slightly before serving.

Nutritional Information

Calories: 250, Protein: 5g, Carbohydrates: 40g, Fat: 8g, Fiber: 5g, Cholesterol: 0 mg, Salt: 150 mg, Potassium: 300 mg

WHOLE-GRAIN WAFFLES WITH FRESH BERRIES

Servings 4 | Prep: 10 min | Cook: 15 min

These heart-healthy whole-grain waffles are light, crispy, and topped with a burst of fresh berries, making them a delightful and nutritious start to your day.

Equipment

Waffle Iron, Mixing Bowl, Whisk

Ingredients

- 200 g whole-grain flour
- 10 g baking powder
- 2 g salt
- 300 ml low-fat milk
- 50 ml olive oil
- 1 egg
- 200 g mixed fresh berries (such as strawberries, blueberries, and raspberries)
- 15 ml honey (optional, for drizzling)

Directions

1. Preheat the waffle iron according to the manufacturer's instructions.
2. In a mixing bowl, whisk together the whole-grain flour, baking powder, and salt.
3. In another bowl, combine the low-fat milk, olive oil, and egg, then mix well.
4. Gradually add the wet ingredients to the dry ingredients, stirring until just combined.
5. Pour the batter onto the preheated waffle iron and cook until golden brown and crisp.
6. Serve the waffles warm, topped with fresh berries and a drizzle of honey if desired.

Nutritional Information

Calories: 280, Protein: 8g, Carbohydrates: 40g, Fat: 10g, Fiber: 6g, Cholesterol: 35 mg, Salt: 300 mg, Potassium: 250 mg

WARM QUINOA PORRIDGE WITH ALMONDS

Servings 4 | Prep: 5 min | Cook: 20 min

This comforting quinoa porridge is a heart-healthy breakfast option, rich in protein and fiber, and topped with crunchy almonds for added texture and flavor.

Equipment

Medium Saucepan, Whisk, Measuring Cups and Spoons

Ingredients

- 200 g Quinoa
- 500 ml Almond Milk
- 30 g Almonds, chopped
- 15 ml Honey
- 5 g Ground Cinnamon
- 2 g Salt
- 5 ml Vanilla Extract

Directions

1. Rinse the quinoa under cold water to remove any bitterness.
2. In a medium saucepan, combine the quinoa, almond milk, and salt. Bring to a boil over medium heat.
3. Reduce the heat to low, cover, and simmer for 15 minutes, or until the quinoa is tender and the liquid is absorbed.
4. Stir in the honey, ground cinnamon, and vanilla extract. Cook for an additional 2 minutes.
5. Serve warm, topped with chopped almonds.

Nutritional Information

Calories: 230, Protein: 7g, Carbohydrates: 35g, Fat: 7g, Fiber: 5g, Cholesterol: 0 mg, Salt: 150 mg, Potassium: 180 mg

GREEK YOGURT PARFAIT WITH MIXED BERRIES

Servings 2 | Prep: 10 min | Cook: 0 min

A refreshing and nutritious start to your day, this Greek yogurt parfait combines creamy yogurt with the natural sweetness of mixed berries and a satisfying crunch from granola.

Equipment

Bowl, Spoon, Glass or Parfait Cup

Ingredients

- 300 g Greek yogurt
- 100 g mixed berries (such as strawberries, blueberries, and raspberries)
- 50 g granola
- 10 ml honey (optional)
- 5 g chia seeds (optional)

Directions

1. Spoon half of the Greek yogurt into the bottom of each glass or parfait cup.
2. Layer half of the mixed berries over the yogurt.
3. Add a layer of granola on top of the berries.
4. Repeat the layers with the remaining yogurt, berries, and granola.
5. Drizzle honey over the top, if desired, and sprinkle with chia seeds for added texture and nutrition.

Nutritional Information

Calories: 250, Protein: 12g, Carbohydrates: 35g, Fat: 8g, Fiber: 5g, Cholesterol: 5 mg, Salt: 50 mg, Potassium: 300 mg

SPINACH AND TOMATO FRITTATA

Servings 4 | Prep: 10 min | Cook: 20 min

This Spinach and Tomato Frittata is a delightful, heart-healthy breakfast option, packed with fresh vegetables and rich in flavor. It's perfect for a nutritious start to your day.

Equipment

Non-stick frying pan, Whisk, Spatula

Ingredients

- 200 g fresh spinach
- 150 g cherry tomatoes, halved
- 6 large eggs
- 50 ml skim milk
- 30 g grated Parmesan cheese
- 1 tbsp olive oil
- Salt and pepper to taste

Directions

1. Preheat the oven to 180°C (356°F).
2. In a non-stick frying pan, heat olive oil over medium heat. Add spinach and sauté until wilted.
3. Add cherry tomatoes to the pan and cook for 2-3 minutes.
4. In a bowl, whisk together eggs, skim milk, Parmesan cheese, salt, and pepper.
5. Pour the egg mixture over the spinach and tomatoes in the pan. Cook on the stove for 5 minutes until the edges start to set.
6. Transfer the pan to the preheated oven and bake for 10-15 minutes, or until the frittata is fully set and slightly golden on top.
7. Allow to cool slightly before slicing and serving.

Nutritional Information

Calories: 180, Protein: 14g, Carbohydrates: 6g, Fat: 11g, Fiber: 2g, Cholesterol: 220 mg, Salt: 250 mg, Potassium: 450 mg

MATCHA CHIA PUDDING

Servings 2 | Prep: 10 min | Cook: 0 min

This Matcha Chia Pudding is a delightful, heart-healthy breakfast option that combines the antioxidant power of matcha with the fiber-rich benefits of chia seeds. It's creamy, subtly sweet, and perfect for a nutritious start to your day.

Equipment

Mixing Bowl, Whisk, Refrigerator

Ingredients

- 30 g Chia Seeds
- 250 ml Unsweetened Almond Milk
- 5 g Matcha Powder
- 10 ml Maple Syrup
- 1 g Vanilla Extract
- 50 g Fresh Berries (for topping)

Directions

1. In a mixing bowl, combine chia seeds, almond milk, matcha powder, maple syrup, and vanilla extract.
2. Whisk the mixture thoroughly until the matcha powder is fully dissolved and the ingredients are well combined.
3. Cover the bowl and refrigerate for at least 2 hours or overnight to allow the chia seeds to absorb the liquid and thicken.
4. Before serving, give the pudding a good stir and divide it into two serving bowls.
5. Top with fresh berries and enjoy your nutritious breakfast.

Nutritional Information

Calories: 180, Protein: 5g, Carbohydrates: 25g, Fat: 8g, Fiber: 10g, Cholesterol: 0 mg, Salt: 50 mg, Potassium: 250 mg

HIGH-FIBER BRAN MUFFINS

Servings 12 | Prep: 15 min | Cook: 20 min

These high-fiber bran muffins are a heart-healthy way to start your day, packed with nutrients and a deliciously wholesome flavor.

Equipment

Mixing Bowl, Muffin Tin, Oven

Ingredients

- 150 g Wheat Bran
- 125 g Whole Wheat Flour
- 100 g Brown Sugar
- 10 g Baking Powder
- 2 g Salt
- 250 ml Low-Fat Milk
- 60 ml Vegetable Oil
- 1 Large Egg
- 100 g Raisins

Directions

1. Preheat the oven to 190°C and lightly grease a muffin tin.
2. In a mixing bowl, combine wheat bran, whole wheat flour, brown sugar, baking powder, and salt.
3. In a separate bowl, whisk together the milk, vegetable oil, and egg.
4. Pour the wet ingredients into the dry ingredients and stir until just combined.
5. Fold in the raisins gently.
6. Spoon the batter evenly into the prepared muffin tin.
7. Bake for 20 minutes or until a toothpick inserted into the center comes out clean.
8. Allow to cool slightly before serving.

Nutritional Information

Calories: 180, Protein: 4g, Carbohydrates: 32g, Fat: 5g, Fiber: 5g, Cholesterol: 15 mg, Salt: 150 mg, Potassium: 200 mg

PEANUT BUTTER AND APPLE SLICES ON RYE TOAST

Servings 2 | Prep: 5 min | Cook: 5 min

This delightful breakfast combines the creamy richness of peanut butter with the crisp sweetness of apples, all atop hearty rye toast. It's a perfect start to your day, offering a balance of flavors and nutrients.

Equipment

Toaster, Knife, Cutting Board

Ingredients

- 4 slices of rye bread (approximately 200g)
- 60g natural peanut butter
- 1 medium apple (approximately 150g), thinly sliced
- 10g honey (optional)
- A pinch of cinnamon (optional)

Directions

1. Toast the rye bread slices in a toaster until golden brown.
2. Spread 15g of peanut butter evenly on each slice of toast.
3. Arrange the apple slices over the peanut butter on each piece of toast.
4. Drizzle a small amount of honey over the apple slices, if desired.
5. Sprinkle a pinch of cinnamon on top for added flavor, if using.

Nutritional Information

Calories: 320, Protein: 9g, Carbohydrates: 45g, Fat: 12g, Fiber: 7g, Cholesterol: 0mg, Salt: 250mg, Potassium: 300mg

BAKED AVOCADO EGG CUPS

Servings 4 | Prep: 10 min | Cook: 15 min

These Baked Avocado Egg Cups are a delicious and nutritious way to start your day, combining creamy avocado with perfectly baked eggs for a heart-healthy breakfast.

Equipment

Oven, Baking Tray, Spoon

Ingredients

- 2 large avocados
- 4 medium eggs
- 10 g chopped fresh chives
- 2 g salt
- 2 g black pepper

Directions

1. Preheat the oven to 200°C.
2. Cut the avocados in half and remove the pits. Scoop out a small amount of flesh to create space for the eggs.
3. Place the avocado halves on a baking tray, ensuring they are stable.
4. Crack an egg into each avocado half, season with salt and pepper.
5. Bake in the oven for 12-15 minutes, until the egg whites are set.
6. Remove from the oven and sprinkle with chopped chives before serving.

Nutritional Information

Calories: 220, Protein: 9g, Carbohydrates: 8g, Fat: 18g, Fiber: 6g, Cholesterol: 186 mg, Salt: 500 mg, Potassium: 690 mg

ZUCCHINI AND CARROT BREAKFAST LOAF

Servings 8 | Prep: 15 min | Cook: 45 min

This moist and flavorful breakfast loaf combines the natural sweetness of carrots and the subtle earthiness of zucchini, making it a perfect heart-healthy start to your day.

Equipment

Loaf Pan, Mixing Bowl, Grater

Ingredients

- 200 g Zucchini, grated
- 150 g Carrots, grated
- 200 g Whole Wheat Flour
- 100 g Rolled Oats
- 100 ml Unsweetened Applesauce
- 2 Large Eggs
- 60 ml Olive Oil
- 100 ml Low-Fat Milk
- 50 g Honey
- 10 g Baking Powder
- 5 g Ground Cinnamon
- 2 g Salt

Directions

1. Preheat the oven to 180°C and grease a loaf pan.
2. In a mixing bowl, combine grated zucchini, carrots, applesauce, eggs, olive oil, milk, and honey. Mix well.
3. In another bowl, whisk together whole wheat flour, rolled oats, baking powder, cinnamon, and salt.
4. Gradually add the dry ingredients to the wet mixture, stirring until just combined.
5. Pour the batter into the prepared loaf pan and smooth the top.
6. Bake for 45 minutes, or until a toothpick inserted into the center comes out clean.
7. Allow the loaf to cool in the pan for 10 minutes before transferring to a wire rack to cool completely.

Nutritional Information

Calories: 210, Protein: 5g, Carbohydrates: 30g, Fat: 8g, Fiber: 4g, Cholesterol: 35 mg, Salt: 150 mg, Potassium: 250 mg

Snacks and Appetizers

ROASTED CHICKPEAS WITH PAPRIKA

Servings 4 | Prep: 10 min | Cook: 30 min

These roasted chickpeas are a crunchy, flavorful snack that's perfect for heart health. Packed with protein and fiber, they're seasoned with paprika for a smoky kick.

Equipment

Baking Tray, Mixing Bowl, Oven

Ingredients

- 400 g Canned Chickpeas, drained and rinsed
- 15 ml Olive Oil
- 5 g Paprika
- 2 g Garlic Powder
- 2 g Salt
- 1 g Black Pepper

Directions

1. Preheat the oven to 200°C (392°F).
2. Pat the chickpeas dry with a paper towel to remove excess moisture.
3. In a mixing bowl, combine chickpeas, olive oil, paprika, garlic powder, salt, and black pepper. Mix well to coat evenly.
4. Spread the chickpeas in a single layer on a baking tray.
5. Roast in the oven for 30 minutes, stirring halfway through, until golden and crispy.
6. Allow to cool slightly before serving.

Nutritional Information

Calories: 150, Protein: 6g, Carbohydrates: 20g, Fat: 5g, Fiber: 6g, Cholesterol: 0 mg, Salt: 150 mg, Potassium: 200 mg

CUCUMBER AND HUMMUS BITES

Servings 4 | Prep: 15 min | Cook: 0 min

These refreshing cucumber and hummus bites are the perfect heart-healthy appetizer, combining the crunch of fresh cucumber with the creamy richness of hummus.

Equipment

Cutting Board, Knife, Measuring Spoons

Ingredients

- 1 large cucumber (approximately 300g)
- 200g hummus
- 50g cherry tomatoes
- 10g fresh parsley
- 5ml lemon juice
- Salt and pepper to taste

Directions

1. Wash the cucumber and slice it into 1 cm thick rounds.
2. Spread approximately 10g of hummus on each cucumber slice.
3. Halve the cherry tomatoes and place one half on top of the hummus.
4. Finely chop the parsley and sprinkle over the cucumber bites.
5. Drizzle with a little lemon juice and season with salt and pepper to taste.

Nutritional Information

Calories: 85, Protein: 3g, Carbohydrates: 10g, Fat: 4g, Fiber: 3g, Cholesterol: 0mg, Salt: 150mg, Potassium: 250mg

AVOCADO DEVILED EGGS

Servings 4 | Prep: 15 min | Cook: 10 min

A creamy and nutritious twist on the classic deviled eggs, these avocado deviled eggs are rich in healthy fats and bursting with flavor, making them a perfect heart-healthy snack.

Equipment

Saucepan, Mixing Bowl, Fork

Ingredients

- 4 large eggs
- 1 ripe avocado (about 150g)
- 10 ml lime juice
- 5 g Dijon mustard
- 2 g garlic powder
- 2 g paprika
- Salt and pepper to taste
- 10 g fresh cilantro, chopped

Directions

1. Place the eggs in a saucepan, cover with water, and bring to a boil. Once boiling, remove from heat and let sit for 10 minutes.
2. Drain and cool the eggs under cold running water. Peel the eggs and slice them in half lengthwise.
3. Scoop out the yolks and place them in a mixing bowl. Add the avocado, lime juice, Dijon mustard, garlic powder, salt, and pepper.
4. Mash the mixture with a fork until smooth and creamy.
5. Spoon or pipe the avocado mixture back into the egg whites.
6. Sprinkle with paprika and garnish with chopped cilantro.

Nutritional Information

Calories: 150, Protein: 7g, Carbohydrates: 6g, Fat: 11g, Fiber: 4g, Cholesterol: 186 mg, Salt: 150 mg, Potassium: 350 mg

BAKED KALE CHIPS WITH GARLIC

Servings 4 | Prep: 10 min | Cook: 15 min

These crispy baked kale chips are a delicious and nutritious snack, infused with the rich flavor of garlic. Perfect for a heart-healthy diet, they offer a satisfying crunch without the guilt.

Equipment

Baking Sheet, Mixing Bowl, Oven

Ingredients

- 200 g Kale Leaves
- 15 ml Olive Oil
- 5 g Garlic Powder
- 2 g Sea Salt
- 1 g Black Pepper

Directions

1. Preheat the oven to 150°C (300°F).
2. Wash and thoroughly dry the kale leaves. Remove the stems and tear the leaves into bite-sized pieces.
3. In a mixing bowl, toss the kale with olive oil, garlic powder, sea salt, and black pepper until evenly coated.
4. Spread the kale pieces in a single layer on a baking sheet.
5. Bake for 15 minutes, or until the edges are brown but not burnt. Check halfway through to ensure even baking.

Nutritional Information

Calories: 60, Protein: 2g, Carbohydrates: 5g, Fat: 4g, Fiber: 2g, Cholesterol: 0 mg, Salt: 150 mg, Potassium: 300 mg

SWEET POTATO HUMMUS WITH VEGGIE STICKS

Servings 4 | Prep: 15 min | Cook: 30 min

This vibrant and creamy sweet potato hummus is a delightful twist on the classic dip, offering a sweet and savory flavor profile that pairs perfectly with crunchy veggie sticks.

Equipment

Baking Sheet, Food Processor, Serving Bowl

Ingredients

- 200 g Sweet Potato, peeled and cubed
- 400 g Canned Chickpeas, drained and rinsed
- 60 ml Olive Oil
- 30 ml Lemon Juice
- 1 clove Garlic, minced
- 5 g Ground Cumin
- 2 g Salt
- 50 ml Water
- Assorted Veggie Sticks (e.g., carrots, cucumbers, bell peppers)

Directions

1. Preheat the oven to 200°C. Place the sweet potato cubes on a baking sheet and roast for 25-30 minutes until tender.
2. In a food processor, combine roasted sweet potato, chickpeas, olive oil, lemon juice, garlic, cumin, and salt.
3. Blend until smooth, gradually adding water to achieve desired consistency.
4. Transfer the hummus to a serving bowl and garnish with a drizzle of olive oil if desired.
5. Serve with assorted veggie sticks for dipping.

Nutritional Information

Calories: 220, Protein: 5g, Carbohydrates: 30g, Fat: 10g, Fiber: 7g, Cholesterol: 0 mg, Salt: 500 mg, Potassium: 450 mg

TOMATO AND BASIL BRUSCHETTA ON WHOLE-GRAIN TOAST

Servings 4 | Prep: 10 min | Cook: 5 min

This delightful bruschetta combines the freshness of ripe tomatoes and aromatic basil on a crunchy whole-grain toast, making it a perfect heart-healthy appetizer.

Equipment

Toaster, Mixing Bowl, Knife

Ingredients

- 4 slices whole-grain bread
- 200 g ripe tomatoes, diced
- 10 g fresh basil leaves, chopped
- 15 ml extra virgin olive oil
- 5 ml balsamic vinegar
- 1 clove garlic, minced
- Salt and pepper to taste

Directions

1. Toast the whole-grain bread slices until golden brown.
2. In a mixing bowl, combine diced tomatoes, chopped basil, olive oil, balsamic vinegar, and minced garlic. Season with salt and pepper.
3. Spoon the tomato mixture evenly over each toasted bread slice.
4. Serve immediately, garnished with extra basil if desired.

Nutritional Information

Calories: 150, Protein: 4g, Carbohydrates: 22g, Fat: 6g, Fiber: 4g, Cholesterol: 0 mg, Salt: 150 mg, Potassium: 300 mg

BAKED ZUCCHINI FRIES

Servings 4 | Prep: 15 min | Cook: 25 min

These crispy baked zucchini fries are a heart-healthy alternative to traditional fries. They are seasoned to perfection and baked until golden, offering a delightful crunch without the guilt.

Equipment

Baking Sheet, Mixing Bowl, Oven

Ingredients

- 400 g zucchini (about 2 medium-sized)
- 100 g whole wheat breadcrumbs
- 50 g grated Parmesan cheese
- 2 large eggs
- 5 g garlic powder
- 5 g onion powder
- 2 g salt
- 2 g black pepper
- 10 ml olive oil spray

Directions

1. Preheat the oven to 220°C (428°F) and line a baking sheet with parchment paper.
2. Cut the zucchini into sticks, about 1 cm thick and 8 cm long.
3. In a mixing bowl, combine breadcrumbs, Parmesan cheese, garlic powder, onion powder, salt, and pepper.
4. Beat the eggs in a separate bowl. Dip each zucchini stick into the egg, then coat with the breadcrumb mixture.
5. Arrange the coated zucchini sticks on the prepared baking sheet and lightly spray with olive oil.
6. Bake for 20-25 minutes, turning halfway through, until golden brown and crispy.

Nutritional Information

Calories: 180, Protein: 10g, Carbohydrates: 20g, Fat: 7g, Fiber: 4g, Cholesterol: 60 mg, Salt: 300 mg, Potassium: 450 mg

ROASTED RED PEPPER AND WALNUT DIP

Servings 6 | Prep: 10 min | Cook: 10 min

This vibrant and creamy dip combines the smoky sweetness of roasted red peppers with the rich, nutty flavor of walnuts. Perfect for a heart-healthy snack or appetizer, it pairs beautifully with whole-grain crackers or fresh vegetable sticks.

Equipment

Blender or Food Processor, Baking Sheet, Spatula

Ingredients

- 300 g roasted red peppers (jarred or homemade)
- 100 g walnuts
- 2 cloves garlic
- 30 ml olive oil
- 15 ml lemon juice
- 5 g ground cumin
- 2 g smoked paprika
- Salt to taste
- Fresh parsley for garnish (optional)

Directions

1. Preheat the oven to 180°C (350°F). Spread walnuts on a baking sheet and toast for 5-7 minutes until fragrant.
2. In a blender or food processor, combine roasted red peppers, toasted walnuts, garlic, olive oil, lemon juice, cumin, smoked paprika, and salt.
3. Blend until smooth, scraping down the sides as needed. Adjust seasoning to taste.
4. Transfer the dip to a serving bowl and garnish with fresh parsley if desired.
5. Serve with whole-grain crackers or fresh vegetable sticks.

Nutritional Information

Calories: 150, Protein: 3g, Carbohydrates: 6g, Fat: 13g, Fiber: 2g, Cholesterol: 0 mg, Salt: 150 mg, Potassium: 200 mg

GREEK YOGURT RANCH DIP WITH CARROTS

Servings 4 | Prep: 10 min | Cook: 0 min

This creamy Greek yogurt ranch dip is a heart-healthy twist on a classic favorite, perfect for pairing with crunchy carrot sticks for a satisfying snack.

Equipment

Mixing Bowl, Whisk, Serving Platter

Ingredients

- 250 g Greek yogurt
- 10 ml lemon juice
- 5 g garlic powder
- 5 g onion powder
- 2 g dried dill
- 2 g dried parsley
- 1 g salt
- 400 g carrots, cut into sticks

Directions

1. In a mixing bowl, combine the Greek yogurt, lemon juice, garlic powder, onion powder, dried dill, dried parsley, and salt.
2. Whisk the ingredients together until smooth and well combined.
3. Transfer the dip to a serving bowl and arrange the carrot sticks on a platter around it.
4. Serve immediately or refrigerate for up to 2 hours to enhance the flavors.
5. Enjoy as a healthy snack or appetizer.

Nutritional Information

Calories: 80, Protein: 5g, Carbohydrates: 12g, Fat: 2g, Fiber: 3g, Cholesterol: 5 mg, Salt: 150 mg, Potassium: 400 mg

EDAMAME WITH SEA SALT AND LEMON

Servings 4 | Prep: 5 min | Cook: 10 min

A simple yet flavorful snack, this dish combines the natural goodness of edamame with a hint of sea salt and a refreshing touch of lemon, perfect for heart-healthy snacking.

Equipment

Steamer or pot with steamer basket, Mixing bowl, Serving dish

Ingredients

- 500 g edamame (in pods)
- 5 g sea salt
- 1 lemon (zested and juiced)

Directions

1. Fill a pot with water and bring to a boil. Place the edamame in a steamer basket over the boiling water.
2. Steam the edamame for about 5-7 minutes until tender and bright green.
3. Transfer the steamed edamame to a mixing bowl.
4. Sprinkle with sea salt and toss to coat evenly.
5. Add lemon zest and juice, tossing again to distribute the flavors.
6. Serve warm in a serving dish.

Nutritional Information

Calories: 120, Protein: 11g, Carbohydrates: 13g, Fat: 5g, Fiber: 5g, Cholesterol: 0 mg, Salt: 300 mg, Potassium: 450 mg

MINI CAPRESE SKEWERS WITH BALSAMIC GLAZE

Servings 4 | Prep: 15 min | Cook: 5 min

These delightful mini Caprese skewers are a fresh and vibrant appetizer, perfect for heart-healthy snacking. The combination of juicy tomatoes, creamy mozzarella, and fragrant basil, drizzled with a tangy balsamic glaze, is both delicious and visually appealing.

Equipment

Skewers, Small Saucepan, Mixing Bowl

Ingredients

- 200 g cherry tomatoes
- 200 g fresh mozzarella balls
- 20 g fresh basil leaves
- 60 ml balsamic vinegar
- 10 ml honey
- 1 g salt
- 1 g black pepper

Directions

1. In a small saucepan, combine balsamic vinegar and honey. Simmer over low heat for about 5 minutes until slightly thickened. Let it cool.
2. Thread one cherry tomato, one mozzarella ball, and one basil leaf onto each skewer. Repeat until all ingredients are used.
3. Arrange skewers on a serving platter.
4. Drizzle the balsamic glaze over the skewers.
5. Season with salt and black pepper to taste.

Nutritional Information

Calories: 150, Protein: 8g, Carbohydrates: 10g, Fat: 9g, Fiber: 1g, Cholesterol: 25 mg, Salt: 150 mg, Potassium: 200 mg

SPICY ROASTED ALMONDS

Servings 4 | Prep: 10 min | Cook: 15 min

These Spicy Roasted Almonds are a perfect heart-healthy snack, offering a satisfying crunch with a kick of spice, ideal for any occasion.

Equipment

Baking Sheet, Mixing Bowl, Oven

Ingredients

- 200 g Raw Almonds
- 15 ml Olive Oil
- 5 g Smoked Paprika
- 3 g Cayenne Pepper
- 2 g Garlic Powder
- 2 g Sea Salt

Directions

1. Preheat the oven to 180°C (350°F).
2. In a mixing bowl, combine olive oil, smoked paprika, cayenne pepper, garlic powder, and sea salt.
3. Add the almonds to the bowl and toss until they are evenly coated with the spice mixture.
4. Spread the almonds in a single layer on a baking sheet.
5. Roast in the preheated oven for 15 minutes, stirring halfway through, until golden and fragrant.
6. Allow to cool before serving or storing in an airtight container.

Nutritional Information

Calories: 210, Protein: 7g, Carbohydrates: 8g, Fat: 18g, Fiber: 4g, Cholesterol: 0 mg, Salt: 150 mg, Potassium: 240 mg

MANGO SALSA WITH BAKED TORTILLA CHIPS

Servings 4 | Prep: 15 min | Cook: 10 min

This vibrant and refreshing mango salsa paired with crispy baked tortilla chips is a heart-healthy snack that bursts with flavor and color. Perfect for a light appetizer or a delightful snack.

Equipment

Baking Sheet, Mixing Bowl, Knife, Cutting Board

Ingredients

- 200 g ripe mango, diced
- 100 g red bell pepper, diced
- 50 g red onion, finely chopped
- 15 g fresh cilantro, chopped
- 1 small jalapeño, seeded and minced
- 30 ml lime juice
- 2 g salt
- 4 whole wheat tortillas
- 10 ml olive oil

Directions

1. Preheat the oven to 180°C (350°F).
2. Cut the whole wheat tortillas into wedges and lightly brush with olive oil.
3. Arrange the tortilla wedges on a baking sheet and bake for 8-10 minutes until golden and crispy.
4. In a mixing bowl, combine the diced mango, red bell pepper, red onion, cilantro, and jalapeño.
5. Add lime juice and salt to the mango mixture, and gently toss to combine.
6. Serve the mango salsa with the baked tortilla chips.

Nutritional Information

Calories: 150, Protein: 3g, Carbohydrates: 28g, Fat: 4g, Fiber: 5g, Cholesterol: 0 mg, Salt: 200 mg, Potassium: 250 mg

WHOLE-WHEAT PITA CHIPS WITH GUACAMOLE

Servings 4 | Prep: 10 min | Cook: 10 min

Enjoy a heart-healthy snack with these crunchy whole-wheat pita chips paired with creamy, nutritious guacamole. Perfect for a quick bite or a party appetizer.

Equipment

Baking Sheet, Mixing Bowl, Knife

Ingredients

- 4 whole-wheat pitas (200 g total)
- 15 ml olive oil
- 2 ripe avocados (300 g total)
- 1 small tomato (100 g), diced
- 30 ml lime juice
- 1 small red onion (50 g), finely chopped
- 5 g fresh cilantro, chopped
- 2 g salt
- 1 g black pepper

Directions

1. Preheat the oven to 180°C (350°F).
2. Cut each pita into 8 wedges and arrange them on a baking sheet.
3. Brush the pita wedges with olive oil and bake for 8-10 minutes until golden and crisp.
4. In a mixing bowl, mash the avocados with lime juice until smooth.
5. Stir in the diced tomato, chopped onion, cilantro, salt, and pepper.
6. Serve the guacamole with the warm pita chips.

Nutritional Information

Calories: 250, Protein: 5g, Carbohydrates: 30g, Fat: 14g, Fiber: 8g, Cholesterol: 0 mg, Salt: 200 mg, Potassium: 500 mg

LENTIL AND SPINACH PATTIES

Servings 4 | Prep: 15 min | Cook: 20 min

These lentil and spinach patties are a delicious and nutritious snack, perfect for heart health. Packed with plant-based protein and fiber, they offer a satisfying crunch with every bite.

Equipment

Mixing Bowl, Frying Pan, Spatula

Ingredients

- 200 g cooked lentils
- 100 g fresh spinach, chopped
- 50 g whole wheat breadcrumbs
- 1 small onion, finely chopped
- 2 cloves garlic, minced
- 5 g ground cumin
- 5 g ground coriander
- 1 egg, beaten
- 15 ml olive oil
- Salt and pepper to taste

Directions

1. In a mixing bowl, combine the cooked lentils, chopped spinach, breadcrumbs, onion, garlic, cumin, coriander, and beaten egg. Season with salt and pepper.
2. Mix the ingredients thoroughly until well combined.
3. Form the mixture into small patties, about 2 cm thick.
4. Heat olive oil in a frying pan over medium heat.
5. Cook the patties for 3-4 minutes on each side, or until golden brown and heated through.
6. Serve warm with a side of yogurt or your favorite dipping sauce.

Nutritional Information

Calories: 180, Protein: 10g, Carbohydrates: 25g, Fat: 5g, Fiber: 8g, Cholesterol: 35 mg, Salt: 150 mg, Potassium: 450 mg

HEART-HEALTHY TRAIL MIX WITH DARK CHOCOLATE

Servings 8 | Prep: 10 min | Cook: 0 min

This trail mix combines the richness of dark chocolate with the crunch of nuts and seeds, offering a heart-healthy snack that's both satisfying and nutritious.

Equipment

Mixing Bowl, Measuring Cups, Airtight Container

Ingredients

- 100 g unsalted almonds
- 100 g unsalted walnuts
- 50 g pumpkin seeds
- 50 g sunflower seeds
- 100 g dried cranberries
- 50 g dark chocolate chips (70% cocoa or higher)

Directions

1. Combine almonds, walnuts, pumpkin seeds, and sunflower seeds in a mixing bowl.
2. Add dried cranberries and dark chocolate chips to the nut and seed mixture.
3. Stir the mixture until all ingredients are evenly distributed.
4. Transfer the trail mix to an airtight container for storage.
5. Enjoy as a snack or pack it for on-the-go energy.

Nutritional Information

Calories: 250, Protein: 6g, Carbohydrates: 20g, Fat: 18g, Fiber: 4g, Cholesterol: 0 mg, Salt: 2 mg, Potassium: 250 mg

STUFFED MUSHROOMS WITH RICOTTA AND HERBS

Servings 4 | Prep: 15 min | Cook: 20 min

These stuffed mushrooms are a delightful blend of creamy ricotta and fresh herbs, offering a heart-healthy appetizer that's both delicious and nutritious.

Equipment

Baking Tray, Mixing Bowl, Spoon

Ingredients

- 400 g Button Mushrooms (stems removed)
- 200 g Ricotta Cheese
- 30 g Fresh Spinach (chopped)
- 10 g Fresh Parsley (chopped)
- 10 g Fresh Basil (chopped)
- 1 clove Garlic (minced)
- 15 ml Olive Oil
- 5 g Lemon Zest
- Salt and Pepper to taste

Directions

1. Preheat the oven to 180°C (350°F).
2. In a mixing bowl, combine ricotta cheese, spinach, parsley, basil, garlic, lemon zest, salt, and pepper. Mix well.
3. Stuff each mushroom cap with the ricotta mixture, pressing gently to fill.
4. Place the stuffed mushrooms on a baking tray and drizzle with olive oil.
5. Bake in the preheated oven for 20 minutes, or until the mushrooms are tender and the tops are lightly golden.

Nutritional Information

Calories: 120, Protein: 7g, Carbohydrates: 8g, Fat: 7g, Fiber: 2g, Cholesterol: 15 mg, Salt: 150 mg, Potassium: 300 mg

AIR-FRIED CAULIFLOWER BUFFALO BITES

Servings 4 | Prep: 15 min | Cook: 20 min

Crispy on the outside and tender on the inside, these cauliflower bites are a spicy, heart-healthy alternative to traditional buffalo wings. Perfect for a snack or appetizer, they deliver all the flavor with none of the guilt.

Equipment

Air Fryer, Mixing Bowl, Whisk

Ingredients

- 500 g Cauliflower, cut into florets
- 100 ml Hot Sauce
- 30 ml Olive Oil
- 50 g Whole Wheat Flour
- 5 g Garlic Powder
- 5 g Onion Powder
- 2 g Paprika
- 2 g Salt
- 1 g Black Pepper

Directions

1. Preheat the air fryer to 200°C.
2. In a mixing bowl, combine flour, garlic powder, onion powder, paprika, salt, and black pepper.
3. Toss cauliflower florets in the flour mixture until evenly coated.
4. Arrange the coated cauliflower in the air fryer basket in a single layer. Air fry for 15 minutes, shaking the basket halfway through.
5. In a separate bowl, whisk together hot sauce and olive oil. Toss the air-fried cauliflower in the sauce until well coated.
6. Return the cauliflower to the air fryer for an additional 5 minutes to crisp up.

Nutritional Information

Calories: 150, Protein: 4g, Carbohydrates: 18g, Fat: 7g, Fiber: 4g, Cholesterol: 0 mg, Salt: 300 mg, Potassium: 400 mg

SMOKED SALMON AND CUCUMBER ROLLS

Servings 4 | Prep: 15 min | Cook: 0 min

These refreshing smoked salmon and cucumber rolls are a delightful heart-healthy appetizer, combining the rich taste of salmon with the crispness of cucumber, perfect for any occasion.

Equipment

Cutting Board, Sharp Knife, Vegetable Peeler

Ingredients

- 200 g Smoked Salmon
- 1 Large Cucumber
- 100 g Low-Fat Cream Cheese
- 1 tbsp Fresh Dill, chopped
- 1 tbsp Lemon Juice
- 1/4 tsp Black Pepper

Directions

1. Peel the cucumber into long, thin strips using a vegetable peeler.
2. In a bowl, mix the cream cheese, lemon juice, dill, and black pepper until smooth.
3. Spread a thin layer of the cream cheese mixture onto each cucumber strip.
4. Place a slice of smoked salmon on top of the cream cheese layer.
5. Roll the cucumber strip tightly and secure with a toothpick if needed.
6. Repeat with the remaining ingredients.
7. Serve chilled and enjoy!

Nutritional Information

Calories: 120, Protein: 10g, Carbohydrates: 4g, Fat: 7g, Fiber: 1g, Cholesterol: 25mg, Salt: 300mg, Potassium: 250mg

BALSAMIC ROASTED BRUSSELS SPROUTS

Servings 4 | Prep: 10 min | Cook: 25 min

These balsamic roasted Brussels sprouts are a delightful blend of tangy and savory flavors, perfect for a heart-healthy snack or appetizer. The roasting process brings out their natural sweetness, making them a crowd-pleaser.

Equipment

Baking Sheet, Mixing Bowl, Oven

Ingredients

- 500 g Brussels sprouts, trimmed and halved
- 30 ml balsamic vinegar
- 15 ml olive oil
- 5 g garlic powder
- 2 g salt
- 2 g black pepper

Directions

1. Preheat the oven to 200°C (392°F).
2. In a mixing bowl, combine Brussels sprouts, balsamic vinegar, olive oil, garlic powder, salt, and black pepper.
3. Toss the Brussels sprouts until they are evenly coated with the mixture.
4. Spread the Brussels sprouts in a single layer on a baking sheet.
5. Roast in the preheated oven for 20-25 minutes, stirring halfway through, until they are tender and caramelized.

Nutritional Information

Calories: 90, Protein: 3g, Carbohydrates: 12g, Fat: 4g, Fiber: 4g, Cholesterol: 0 mg, Salt: 500 mg, Potassium: 350 mg

ALMOND BUTTER AND DATE ENERGY BITES

Servings 12 | Prep: 15 min | Cook: 0 min

These Almond Butter and Date Energy Bites are a perfect heart-healthy snack, packed with natural sweetness and protein. They're easy to make and perfect for on-the-go energy.

Equipment

Food Processor, Mixing Bowl, Measuring Cups

Ingredients

- 200 g Pitted Dates
- 100 g Almond Butter
- 50 g Rolled Oats
- 30 g Chia Seeds
- 20 g Unsweetened Cocoa Powder
- 10 g Flaxseed Meal
- 5 ml Vanilla Extract

Directions

1. Place the pitted dates in the food processor and pulse until they form a sticky paste.
2. Add almond butter, rolled oats, chia seeds, cocoa powder, flaxseed meal, and vanilla extract to the processor.
3. Pulse until all ingredients are well combined and form a dough-like consistency.
4. Transfer the mixture to a mixing bowl.
5. Roll the mixture into 12 equal-sized balls using your hands.
6. Place the energy bites on a tray and refrigerate for at least 30 minutes before serving.

Nutritional Information

Calories: 120, Protein: 3g, Carbohydrates: 15g, Fat: 6g, Fiber: 4g, Cholesterol: 0 mg, Salt: 2 mg, Potassium: 180 mg

MASHED AVOCADO ON RYE CRACKERS

Servings 4 | Prep: 10 min | Cook: 0 min

This heart-healthy snack combines creamy avocado with the robust flavor of rye crackers, offering a satisfying crunch and a burst of freshness.

Equipment

Mixing Bowl, Fork, Knife

Ingredients

- 200 g Avocado (about 1 large avocado)
- 100 g Rye Crackers (approximately 8 crackers)
- 10 ml Fresh Lime Juice
- 5 g Fresh Cilantro, chopped
- 2 g Salt
- 1 g Black Pepper
- 20 g Cherry Tomatoes, diced

Directions

1. Cut the avocado in half, remove the pit, and scoop the flesh into a mixing bowl.
2. Add lime juice, salt, and black pepper to the avocado. Mash with a fork until smooth but slightly chunky.
3. Stir in the chopped cilantro and diced cherry tomatoes.
4. Spread the mashed avocado mixture evenly over each rye cracker.
5. Serve immediately for the best texture and flavor.

Nutritional Information

Calories: 180, Protein: 3g, Carbohydrates: 20g, Fat: 10g, Fiber: 6g, Cholesterol: 0 mg, Salt: 150 mg, Potassium: 350 mg

GARLIC AND HERB ROASTED CASHEWS

Servings 4 | Prep: 10 min | Cook: 15 min

These roasted cashews are infused with the rich flavors of garlic and herbs, offering a heart-healthy snack that's both savory and satisfying.

Equipment

Baking Sheet, Mixing Bowl, Oven

Ingredients

- 200 g Raw Cashews
- 15 ml Olive Oil
- 5 g Garlic Powder
- 5 g Dried Rosemary
- 5 g Dried Thyme
- 2 g Sea Salt
- 1 g Black Pepper

Directions

1. Preheat the oven to 180°C (350°F).
2. In a mixing bowl, combine olive oil, garlic powder, rosemary, thyme, sea salt, and black pepper.
3. Add the cashews to the bowl and toss until they are evenly coated with the herb mixture.
4. Spread the cashews in a single layer on a baking sheet.
5. Roast in the preheated oven for 12-15 minutes, stirring halfway through, until golden brown.
6. Allow to cool slightly before serving.

Nutritional Information

Calories: 220, Protein: 6g, Carbohydrates: 14g, Fat: 18g, Fiber: 2g, Cholesterol: 0 mg, Salt: 150 mg, Potassium: 200 mg

GRILLED EGGPLANT WITH LEMON AND OLIVE OIL

Servings 4 | Prep: 10 min | Cook: 15 min

This simple yet flavorful dish highlights the natural sweetness of eggplant, enhanced by a zesty lemon and olive oil dressing. Perfect as a light appetizer or a healthy snack.

Equipment

Grill pan, Mixing bowl, Basting brush

Ingredients

- 500 g Eggplant, sliced into 1 cm rounds
- 30 ml Olive oil
- 1 Lemon, juiced
- 2 cloves Garlic, minced
- 5 g Fresh parsley, chopped
- Salt and pepper to taste

Directions

1. Preheat the grill pan over medium heat.
2. In a mixing bowl, combine olive oil, lemon juice, minced garlic, salt, and pepper.
3. Brush the eggplant slices with the olive oil mixture on both sides.
4. Grill the eggplant slices for about 5-7 minutes on each side until tender and grill marks appear.
5. Remove from the grill and sprinkle with fresh parsley before serving.

Nutritional Information

Calories: 120, Protein: 2g, Carbohydrates: 10g, Fat: 9g, Fiber: 4g, Cholesterol: 0 mg, Salt: 150 mg, Potassium: 350 mg

SPICED PUMPKIN SEEDS

Servings 4 | Prep: 10 min | Cook: 20 min

These crunchy spiced pumpkin seeds are a perfect heart-healthy snack, offering a delightful blend of savory and spicy flavors.

Equipment

Baking Sheet, Mixing Bowl, Oven

Ingredients

- 200 g Pumpkin Seeds
- 15 ml Olive Oil
- 5 g Paprika
- 3 g Garlic Powder
- 2 g Ground Cumin
- 1 g Cayenne Pepper (optional, for extra heat)
- 2 g Salt

Directions

1. Preheat the oven to 150°C (300°F).
2. In a mixing bowl, combine pumpkin seeds, olive oil, paprika, garlic powder, ground cumin, cayenne pepper, and salt. Mix well to coat the seeds evenly.
3. Spread the seasoned seeds in a single layer on a baking sheet.
4. Bake for 20 minutes, stirring halfway through, until the seeds are golden and crispy.
5. Allow to cool before serving or storing in an airtight container.

Nutritional Information

Calories: 180, Protein: 8g, Carbohydrates: 5g, Fat: 15g, Fiber: 3g, Cholesterol: 0 mg, Salt: 150 mg, Potassium: 200 mg

GREEK YOGURT WITH HONEY AND WALNUTS

Servings 4 | Prep: 10 min | Cook: 0 min

This delightful snack combines creamy Greek yogurt with the natural sweetness of honey and the crunch of walnuts, offering a heart-healthy treat that's both satisfying and nutritious.

Equipment

Mixing Bowl, Spoon, Serving Bowls

Ingredients

- 500 g Greek yogurt
- 60 ml honey
- 80 g walnuts, chopped
- 1 tsp cinnamon (optional)

Directions

1. Divide the Greek yogurt evenly among four serving bowls.
2. Drizzle 15 ml of honey over each serving of yogurt.
3. Sprinkle 20 g of chopped walnuts on top of each bowl.
4. Optionally, dust with a pinch of cinnamon for added flavor.
5. Serve immediately and enjoy this heart-healthy snack.

Nutritional Information

Calories: 250, Protein: 10g, Carbohydrates: 30g, Fat: 12g, Fiber: 2g, Cholesterol: 5 mg, Salt: 60 mg, Potassium: 250 mg

Salads and Sides

QUINOA AND KALE SALAD WITH LEMON DRESSING

Servings 4 | Prep: 15 min | Cook: 15 min

This vibrant salad combines the nutty flavor of quinoa with the earthy taste of kale, all brought together by a zesty lemon dressing. It's a refreshing and nutritious dish perfect for a heart-healthy meal.

Equipment

Medium Saucepan, Large Mixing Bowl, Whisk

Ingredients

- 200 g Quinoa
- 500 ml Water
- 150 g Kale, chopped
- 100 g Cherry Tomatoes, halved
- 50 g Red Onion, thinly sliced
- 30 ml Olive Oil
- 30 ml Lemon Juice
- 5 g Lemon Zest
- 5 g Honey
- 2 g Salt
- 1 g Black Pepper

Directions

1. Rinse the quinoa under cold water. In a medium saucepan, combine quinoa and water. Bring to a boil, then reduce heat and simmer for 15 minutes or until water is absorbed. Fluff with a fork and let cool.
2. In a large mixing bowl, combine the cooled quinoa, kale, cherry tomatoes, and red onion.
3. In a small bowl, whisk together olive oil, lemon juice, lemon zest, honey, salt, and black pepper to make the dressing.
4. Pour the dressing over the quinoa mixture and toss gently to combine.
5. Serve immediately or refrigerate for 30 minutes to allow flavors to meld.

Nutritional Information

Calories: 250, Protein: 7g, Carbohydrates: 35g, Fat: 10g, Fiber: 5g, Cholesterol: 0 mg, Salt: 500 mg, Potassium: 450 mg

MEDITERRANEAN CHICKPEA SALAD

Servings 4 | Prep: 15 min | Cook: 0 min

This vibrant Mediterranean Chickpea Salad is a refreshing and nutritious dish, perfect for a heart-healthy diet. Packed with protein-rich chickpeas, fresh vegetables, and a zesty dressing, it's a delightful addition to any meal.

Equipment

Mixing Bowl, Whisk, Cutting Board

Ingredients

- 400 g Chickpeas, canned and drained
- 150 g Cherry Tomatoes, halved
- 100 g Cucumber, diced
- 50 g Red Onion, finely chopped
- 50 g Kalamata Olives, pitted and sliced
- 30 g Feta Cheese, crumbled
- 15 ml Olive Oil
- 15 ml Lemon Juice
- 5 g Fresh Parsley, chopped
- 2 g Dried Oregano
- Salt and Pepper to taste

Directions

1. In a large mixing bowl, combine chickpeas, cherry tomatoes, cucumber, red onion, and olives.
2. In a small bowl, whisk together olive oil, lemon juice, parsley, oregano, salt, and pepper to create the dressing.
3. Pour the dressing over the chickpea mixture and toss gently to combine.
4. Add the crumbled feta cheese and give it a final toss.
5. Serve immediately or refrigerate for 30 minutes to allow flavors to meld.

Nutritional Information

Calories: 220, Protein: 8g, Carbohydrates: 28g, Fat: 9g, Fiber: 7g, Cholesterol: 10mg, Salt: 300mg, Potassium: 400mg

ROASTED BEET AND ARUGULA SALAD

Servings 4 | Prep: 15 min | Cook: 45 min

This vibrant salad combines the earthy sweetness of roasted beets with the peppery bite of arugula, creating a heart-healthy dish that's as nutritious as it is delicious.

Equipment

Oven, Baking Sheet, Mixing Bowl

Ingredients

- 500 g Beets, peeled and quartered
- 30 ml Olive Oil
- 100 g Arugula
- 50 g Walnuts, toasted
- 50 g Goat Cheese, crumbled
- 30 ml Balsamic Vinegar
- Salt and Pepper to taste

Directions

1. Preheat the oven to 200°C.
2. Toss the beets with olive oil, salt, and pepper, then spread them on a baking sheet.
3. Roast the beets for 40-45 minutes, or until tender. Let them cool slightly.
4. In a mixing bowl, combine the roasted beets, arugula, walnuts, and goat cheese.
5. Drizzle with balsamic vinegar and toss gently to combine.
6. Season with additional salt and pepper to taste before serving.

Nutritional Information

Calories: 220, Protein: 6g, Carbohydrates: 18g, Fat: 15g, Fiber: 4g, Cholesterol: 8mg, Salt: 150mg, Potassium: 500mg

LENTIL AND SPINACH SALAD WITH BALSAMIC VINAIGRETTE

Servings 4 | Prep: 15 min | Cook: 25 min

This vibrant salad combines the earthy flavors of lentils with fresh spinach and a tangy balsamic vinaigrette, making it a perfect heart-healthy side dish.

Equipment

Medium Saucepan, Large Mixing Bowl, Whisk

Ingredients

- 200 g Lentils
- 150 g Fresh Spinach
- 1 Medium Red Onion, finely chopped
- 100 g Cherry Tomatoes, halved
- 50 g Walnuts, toasted and chopped
- 60 ml Balsamic Vinegar
- 30 ml Olive Oil
- 1 Garlic Clove, minced
- Salt and Pepper to taste

Directions

1. Rinse the lentils under cold water. In a medium saucepan, combine lentils with 500 ml of water. Bring to a boil, then reduce heat and simmer for 20-25 minutes until tender. Drain and let cool.
2. In a large mixing bowl, combine the cooled lentils, spinach, red onion, cherry tomatoes, and walnuts.
3. In a small bowl, whisk together balsamic vinegar, olive oil, minced garlic, salt, and pepper to make the vinaigrette.
4. Pour the vinaigrette over the salad and toss gently to combine.
5. Serve immediately or refrigerate for up to 2 hours to allow flavors to meld.

Nutritional Information

Calories: 290, Protein: 12g, Carbohydrates: 28g, Fat: 15g, Fiber: 10g, Cholesterol: 0 mg, Salt: 150 mg, Potassium: 600 mg

AVOCADO AND TOMATO SALAD WITH OLIVE OIL

Servings 4 | Prep: 15 min | Cook: 0 min

This vibrant salad combines creamy avocados and juicy tomatoes, enhanced by the rich flavor of olive oil, making it a heart-healthy delight.

Equipment

Cutting Board, Knife, Mixing Bowl

Ingredients

- 200 g Avocado (about 2 medium avocados)
- 300 g Tomatoes (about 3 medium tomatoes)
- 50 g Red Onion
- 30 ml Extra Virgin Olive Oil
- 10 ml Lemon Juice
- 5 g Fresh Basil Leaves
- 2 g Salt
- 1 g Black Pepper

Directions

1. Dice the avocados and tomatoes into bite-sized pieces and place them in a mixing bowl.
2. Thinly slice the red onion and add it to the bowl with the avocados and tomatoes.
3. Drizzle the extra virgin olive oil and lemon juice over the salad ingredients.
4. Gently toss the salad to combine all ingredients evenly.
5. Tear the fresh basil leaves and sprinkle them over the salad.
6. Season with salt and black pepper to taste, and give it a final gentle toss.

Nutritional Information

Calories: 210, Protein: 2g, Carbohydrates: 12g, Fat: 18g, Fiber: 7g, Cholesterol: 0 mg, Salt: 200 mg, Potassium: 600 mg

RAINBOW SLAW WITH CITRUS DRESSING

Servings 4 | Prep: 15 min | Cook: 0 min

This vibrant and crunchy slaw is a feast for the eyes and a delight for the heart. Packed with colorful vegetables and a zesty citrus dressing, it's a refreshing side dish perfect for any meal.

Equipment

Large Mixing Bowl, Whisk, Grater

Ingredients

- 200 g red cabbage, thinly sliced
- 150 g green cabbage, thinly sliced
- 100 g carrots, grated
- 100 g red bell pepper, thinly sliced
- 50 g fresh parsley, chopped
- 60 ml fresh orange juice
- 30 ml fresh lime juice
- 15 ml olive oil
- 5 g honey
- 2 g salt
- 1 g black pepper

Directions

1. In a large mixing bowl, combine the red cabbage, green cabbage, carrots, red bell pepper, and parsley.
2. In a separate bowl, whisk together the orange juice, lime juice, olive oil, honey, salt, and black pepper to create the dressing.
3. Pour the citrus dressing over the vegetable mixture.
4. Toss everything together until the slaw is well coated with the dressing.
5. Let the slaw sit for at least 10 minutes before serving to allow the flavors to meld.

Nutritional Information

Calories: 85, Protein: 2g, Carbohydrates: 15g, Fat: 3g, Fiber: 4g, Cholesterol: 0 mg, Salt: 200 mg, Potassium: 350 mg

GRILLED ASPARAGUS WITH LEMON ZEST

Servings 4 | Prep: 10 min | Cook: 10 min

This simple yet flavorful dish highlights the natural taste of asparagus, enhanced with a zesty lemon finish. Perfect as a side for any heart-healthy meal.

Equipment

Grill pan, Zester, Tongs

Ingredients

- 500 g Asparagus, trimmed
- 15 ml Olive oil
- 1 Lemon, zested
- 2 g Salt
- 1 g Black pepper
- 10 g Fresh parsley, chopped

Directions

1. Preheat the grill pan over medium heat.
2. Toss the asparagus with olive oil, salt, and black pepper in a bowl.
3. Place the asparagus on the grill pan and cook for 8-10 minutes, turning occasionally, until tender and slightly charred.
4. Transfer the grilled asparagus to a serving platter.
5. Sprinkle lemon zest and fresh parsley over the asparagus before serving.

Nutritional Information

Calories: 70, Protein: 3g, Carbohydrates: 6g, Fat: 4g, Fiber: 3g, Cholesterol: 0 mg, Salt: 200 mg, Potassium: 250 mg

SWEET POTATO AND BLACK BEAN SALAD

Servings 4 | Prep: 15 min | Cook: 25 min

A vibrant and nutritious salad that combines the natural sweetness of roasted sweet potatoes with the hearty texture of black beans, all tossed in a zesty lime dressing. Perfect as a side dish or a light main course.

Equipment

Oven, Baking Sheet, Mixing Bowl

Ingredients

- 500 g sweet potatoes, peeled and diced
- 15 ml olive oil
- 1 g salt
- 1 g black pepper
- 400 g canned black beans, drained and rinsed
- 150 g cherry tomatoes, halved
- 50 g red onion, finely chopped
- 30 ml lime juice
- 10 g fresh cilantro, chopped

Directions

1. Preheat the oven to 200°C.
2. Toss the diced sweet potatoes with olive oil, salt, and pepper. Spread them evenly on a baking sheet.
3. Roast in the oven for 20-25 minutes, or until tender and slightly caramelized.
4. In a large mixing bowl, combine the roasted sweet potatoes, black beans, cherry tomatoes, and red onion.
5. Drizzle with lime juice and sprinkle with chopped cilantro. Toss gently to combine.

Nutritional Information

Calories: 250, Protein: 8g, Carbohydrates: 45g, Fat: 5g, Fiber: 10g, Cholesterol: 0 mg, Salt: 200 mg, Potassium: 800 mg

CUCUMBER, TOMATO, AND FETA SALAD

Servings 4 | Prep: 15 min | Cook: 0 min

This refreshing salad combines crisp cucumbers, juicy tomatoes, and tangy feta cheese, making it a perfect heart-healthy side dish.

Equipment

Mixing Bowl, Cutting Board, Knife

Ingredients

- 300 g Cucumber, sliced
- 200 g Cherry Tomatoes, halved
- 100 g Feta Cheese, crumbled
- 50 g Red Onion, thinly sliced
- 30 ml Olive Oil
- 15 ml Lemon Juice
- 5 g Fresh Dill, chopped
- 2 g Salt
- 1 g Black Pepper

Directions

1. In a mixing bowl, combine the cucumber slices, cherry tomato halves, and red onion slices.
2. Drizzle olive oil and lemon juice over the vegetables.
3. Add crumbled feta cheese and chopped dill to the bowl.
4. Season with salt and black pepper.
5. Gently toss all ingredients until well combined.
6. Serve immediately or chill in the refrigerator for 10 minutes before serving.

Nutritional Information

Calories: 150, Protein: 5g, Carbohydrates: 10g, Fat: 10g, Fiber: 2g, Cholesterol: 15 mg, Salt: 300 mg, Potassium: 350 mg

WARM FARRO SALAD WITH ROASTED VEGETABLES

Servings 4 | Prep: 15 min | Cook: 30 min

This hearty and nutritious salad combines chewy farro with a medley of roasted vegetables, offering a warm and satisfying dish perfect for any meal.

Equipment

Baking sheet, Saucepan, Mixing bowl

Ingredients

- 200 g farro
- 1 l water
- 200 g cherry tomatoes, halved
- 1 red bell pepper, diced
- 1 zucchini, sliced
- 2 tablespoons olive oil
- 1 teaspoon dried oregano
- Salt and pepper to taste
- 50 g arugula
- 30 ml balsamic vinegar

Directions

1. Preheat the oven to 200°C.
2. In a saucepan, bring water to a boil, add farro, and cook for 20-25 minutes until tender. Drain and set aside.
3. On a baking sheet, toss cherry tomatoes, bell pepper, and zucchini with olive oil, oregano, salt, and pepper. Roast for 20 minutes.
4. In a mixing bowl, combine cooked farro, roasted vegetables, and arugula.
5. Drizzle with balsamic vinegar, toss gently, and serve warm.

Nutritional Information

Calories: 320, Protein: 8g, Carbohydrates: 50g, Fat: 10g, Fiber: 8g, Cholesterol: 0 mg, Salt: 150 mg, Potassium: 600 mg

GARLIC AND HERB ROASTED CAULIFLOWER

Servings 4 | Prep: 10 min | Cook: 25 min

This roasted cauliflower dish is infused with garlic and fresh herbs, offering a flavorful and heart-healthy side that complements any meal.

Equipment

Oven, Baking Sheet, Mixing Bowl

Ingredients

- 1 kg Cauliflower, cut into florets
- 30 ml Olive Oil
- 4 cloves Garlic, minced
- 5 g Fresh Rosemary, chopped
- 5 g Fresh Thyme, chopped
- 2 g Salt
- 1 g Black Pepper

Directions

1. Preheat the oven to 200°C (392°F).
2. In a mixing bowl, combine olive oil, minced garlic, rosemary, thyme, salt, and pepper.
3. Add cauliflower florets to the bowl and toss until evenly coated with the herb mixture.
4. Spread the cauliflower in a single layer on a baking sheet.
5. Roast in the oven for 25 minutes, or until the cauliflower is golden brown and tender.
6. Serve warm, garnished with additional fresh herbs if desired.

Nutritional Information

Calories: 120, Protein: 4g, Carbohydrates: 10g, Fat: 8g, Fiber: 4g, Cholesterol: 0 mg, Salt: 200 mg, Potassium: 450 mg

BROCCOLI AND ALMOND SALAD WITH YOGURT DRESSING

Servings 4 | Prep: 15 min | Cook: 5 min

This vibrant salad combines crunchy broccoli and almonds with a creamy yogurt dressing, offering a delightful mix of textures and flavors that are both heart-healthy and satisfying.

Equipment

Mixing Bowl, Whisk, Saucepan

Ingredients

- 500 g Broccoli, cut into small florets
- 100 g Almonds, sliced
- 150 ml Plain Greek Yogurt
- 30 ml Lemon Juice
- 10 ml Olive Oil
- 1 Garlic Clove, minced
- 5 g Honey
- Salt and Pepper, to taste

Directions

1. Blanch the broccoli florets in boiling water for 2 minutes, then drain and rinse under cold water to stop cooking.
2. Toast the sliced almonds in a dry saucepan over medium heat until golden brown, about 3 minutes.
3. In a mixing bowl, whisk together the yogurt, lemon juice, olive oil, minced garlic, and honey until smooth. Season with salt and pepper.
4. Combine the blanched broccoli and toasted almonds in a large bowl.
5. Pour the yogurt dressing over the broccoli and almonds, tossing gently to coat evenly.
6. Serve immediately or refrigerate for up to 2 hours to allow flavors to meld.

Nutritional Information

Calories: 180, Protein: 8g, Carbohydrates: 12g, Fat: 12g, Fiber: 5g, Cholesterol: 2mg, Salt: 150mg, Potassium: 450mg

CARROT AND GINGER SLAW

Servings 4 | Prep: 15 min | Cook: 0 min

This vibrant and refreshing slaw combines the natural sweetness of carrots with the zing of fresh ginger, making it a perfect heart-healthy side dish.

Equipment

Mixing Bowl, Grater, Whisk

Ingredients

- 300 g Carrots, grated
- 20 g Fresh Ginger, grated
- 50 g Red Cabbage, thinly sliced
- 30 ml Apple Cider Vinegar
- 15 ml Olive Oil
- 10 ml Honey
- 5 g Fresh Coriander, chopped
- Salt, to taste
- Pepper, to taste

Directions

1. In a mixing bowl, combine the grated carrots, ginger, and sliced red cabbage.
2. In a separate small bowl, whisk together the apple cider vinegar, olive oil, and honey until well combined.
3. Pour the dressing over the carrot mixture and toss to coat evenly.
4. Add the chopped coriander and season with salt and pepper to taste.
5. Let the slaw sit for at least 10 minutes to allow the flavors to meld before serving.

Nutritional Information

Calories: 85, Protein: 1.2g, Carbohydrates: 12g, Fat: 4g, Fiber: 3g, Cholesterol: 0 mg, Salt: 150 mg, Potassium: 320 mg

WILD RICE AND CRANBERRY PILAF

Servings 4 | Prep: 10 min | Cook: 45 min

This vibrant Wild Rice and Cranberry Pilaf is a delightful blend of nutty wild rice, sweet cranberries, and crunchy almonds, perfect as a heart-healthy side dish.

Equipment

Medium Saucepan, Strainer, Mixing Bowl

Ingredients

- 200 g Wild Rice
- 750 ml Water
- 100 g Dried Cranberries
- 50 g Sliced Almonds
- 1 Medium Onion, finely chopped
- 15 ml Olive Oil
- 5 g Fresh Parsley, chopped
- Salt and Pepper to taste

Directions

1. Rinse the wild rice under cold water using a strainer.
2. In a medium saucepan, bring water to a boil, add the wild rice, and reduce heat to low. Cover and simmer for 40-45 minutes until rice is tender.
3. In a mixing bowl, combine dried cranberries and sliced almonds.
4. In a separate pan, heat olive oil over medium heat, add chopped onion, and sauté until translucent.
5. Combine cooked wild rice, sautéed onions, cranberries, and almonds. Mix well and season with salt and pepper.
6. Garnish with fresh parsley before serving.

Nutritional Information

Calories: 320, Protein: 7g, Carbohydrates: 50g, Fat: 10g, Fiber: 5g, Cholesterol: 0 mg, Salt: 150 mg, Potassium: 250 mg

SPINACH AND STRAWBERRY SALAD WITH WALNUTS

Servings 4 | Prep: 15 min | Cook: 0 min

This vibrant salad combines the sweetness of strawberries with the earthiness of spinach and the crunch of walnuts, creating a refreshing and heart-healthy dish perfect for any meal.

Equipment

Large Salad Bowl, Small Mixing Bowl, Whisk

Ingredients

- 200 g Fresh Spinach Leaves
- 150 g Strawberries, hulled and sliced
- 50 g Walnuts, roughly chopped
- 50 g Feta Cheese, crumbled (optional)
- 30 ml Balsamic Vinegar
- 15 ml Olive Oil
- 5 g Honey
- Salt and Pepper to taste

Directions

1. In a large salad bowl, combine the spinach leaves, sliced strawberries, and chopped walnuts.
2. If using, sprinkle the crumbled feta cheese over the salad mixture.
3. In a small mixing bowl, whisk together the balsamic vinegar, olive oil, honey, salt, and pepper until well combined.
4. Drizzle the dressing over the salad and gently toss to ensure even coating.
5. Serve immediately, garnished with additional walnuts or strawberries if desired.

Nutritional Information

Calories: 180, Protein: 4g, Carbohydrates: 12g, Fat: 14g, Fiber: 3g, Cholesterol: 5 mg, Salt: 120 mg, Potassium: 400 mg

ROASTED BRUSSELS SPROUTS WITH POMEGRANATE SEEDS

Servings 4 | Prep: 10 min | Cook: 25 min

This vibrant dish combines the earthy flavors of roasted Brussels sprouts with the sweet-tart burst of pomegranate seeds, creating a delightful and heart-healthy side dish.

Equipment

Oven, Baking Sheet, Mixing Bowl

Ingredients

- 500 g Brussels sprouts, trimmed and halved
- 30 ml olive oil
- 2 g salt
- 1 g black pepper
- 100 g pomegranate seeds
- 10 g fresh parsley, chopped

Directions

1. Preheat the oven to 200°C (392°F).
2. In a mixing bowl, toss the Brussels sprouts with olive oil, salt, and black pepper until evenly coated.
3. Spread the Brussels sprouts in a single layer on a baking sheet.
4. Roast in the oven for 20-25 minutes, or until they are golden brown and tender.
5. Remove from the oven and transfer to a serving dish.
6. Sprinkle with pomegranate seeds and fresh parsley before serving.

Nutritional Information

Calories: 150, Protein: 4g, Carbohydrates: 20g, Fat: 7g, Fiber: 6g, Cholesterol: 0 mg, Salt: 500 mg, Potassium: 500 mg

MARINATED ARTICHOKES AND OLIVES

Servings 4 | Prep: 15 min | Cook: 0 min

This vibrant and tangy salad combines the earthy flavors of artichokes with the briny taste of olives, creating a delightful side dish perfect for heart-healthy dining.

Equipment

Mixing Bowl, Whisk, Measuring Cups

Ingredients

- 200 g Artichoke Hearts, quartered
- 100 g Mixed Olives, pitted
- 50 g Red Onion, thinly sliced
- 30 ml Extra Virgin Olive Oil
- 15 ml Lemon Juice
- 5 g Fresh Parsley, chopped
- 2 g Dried Oregano
- Salt and Pepper, to taste

Directions

1. In a mixing bowl, combine the artichoke hearts, mixed olives, and red onion.
2. In a separate small bowl, whisk together the olive oil, lemon juice, parsley, oregano, salt, and pepper.
3. Pour the dressing over the artichoke and olive mixture, tossing gently to coat.
4. Let the salad marinate for at least 10 minutes to allow the flavors to meld.
5. Serve chilled or at room temperature, garnished with additional parsley if desired.

Nutritional Information

Calories: 150, Protein: 2g, Carbohydrates: 8g, Fat: 12g, Fiber: 4g, Cholesterol: 0 mg, Salt: 300 mg, Potassium: 150 mg

GRILLED ZUCCHINI AND RED PEPPERS

Servings 4 | Prep: 10 min | Cook: 15 min

This vibrant and flavorful dish combines the smoky taste of grilled vegetables with a hint of garlic and herbs, making it a perfect heart-healthy side.

Equipment

Grill, Mixing Bowl, Tongs

Ingredients

- 400 g Zucchini, sliced into rounds
- 300 g Red Bell Peppers, sliced into strips
- 30 ml Olive Oil
- 2 cloves Garlic, minced
- 5 g Fresh Basil, chopped
- 2 g Salt
- 1 g Black Pepper

Directions

1. Preheat the grill to medium-high heat.
2. In a mixing bowl, combine olive oil, minced garlic, salt, and black pepper.
3. Add zucchini and red bell peppers to the bowl and toss to coat evenly with the oil mixture.
4. Place the vegetables on the grill and cook for 5-7 minutes on each side, until tender and slightly charred.
5. Remove from the grill and sprinkle with fresh basil before serving.

Nutritional Information

Calories: 120, Protein: 2g, Carbohydrates: 8g, Fat: 9g, Fiber: 3g, Cholesterol: 0 mg, Salt: 200 mg, Potassium: 450 mg

WATERMELON AND FETA SALAD WITH MINT

Servings 4 | Prep: 15 min | Cook: 0 min

This refreshing salad combines juicy watermelon, creamy feta, and aromatic mint for a delightful balance of sweet and savory flavors, perfect for a heart-healthy side dish.

Equipment

Large Mixing Bowl, Knife, Cutting Board

Ingredients

- 600 g Watermelon, cubed
- 150 g Feta Cheese, crumbled
- 30 g Fresh Mint Leaves, chopped
- 50 g Red Onion, thinly sliced
- 30 ml Extra Virgin Olive Oil
- 15 ml Fresh Lime Juice
- 1 g Black Pepper, freshly ground

Directions

1. In a large mixing bowl, combine the watermelon cubes, crumbled feta cheese, and chopped mint leaves.
2. Add the thinly sliced red onion to the bowl.
3. Drizzle the extra virgin olive oil and fresh lime juice over the salad ingredients.
4. Gently toss the salad to ensure all ingredients are evenly coated with the dressing.
5. Season with freshly ground black pepper to taste.
6. Serve immediately or chill in the refrigerator for 10 minutes before serving for a cooler option.

Nutritional Information

Calories: 180, Protein: 6g, Carbohydrates: 20g, Fat: 10g, Fiber: 2g, Cholesterol: 25 mg, Salt: 300 mg, Potassium: 350 mg

TOMATO AND WHITE BEAN SALAD

Servings 4 | Prep: 15 min | Cook: 0 min

This vibrant and refreshing salad combines juicy tomatoes with creamy white beans, offering a delightful blend of flavors and textures. Perfect as a side dish or a light meal, it's both heart-healthy and satisfying.

Equipment

Mixing Bowl, Measuring Cups, Spoon

Ingredients

- 400 g canned white beans, drained and rinsed
- 300 g cherry tomatoes, halved
- 50 g red onion, finely chopped
- 30 ml extra virgin olive oil
- 15 ml balsamic vinegar
- 10 g fresh basil leaves, chopped
- Salt and pepper to taste

Directions

1. In a mixing bowl, combine the white beans, cherry tomatoes, and red onion.
2. Drizzle the olive oil and balsamic vinegar over the salad.
3. Gently toss the ingredients to ensure even coating.
4. Add the chopped basil leaves and season with salt and pepper to taste.
5. Toss again lightly and serve immediately or chill for 10 minutes for enhanced flavors.

Nutritional Information

Calories: 180, Protein: 7g, Carbohydrates: 25g, Fat: 6g, Fiber: 6g, Cholesterol: 0 mg, Salt: 150 mg, Potassium: 450 mg

CABBAGE AND APPLE SLAW

Servings 4 | Prep: 15 min | Cook: 0 min

This refreshing cabbage and apple slaw is a delightful blend of crunchy and sweet, perfect as a side dish to complement any heart-healthy meal.

Equipment

Mixing Bowl, Whisk, Knife, Cutting Board

Ingredients

- 300 g Green Cabbage, thinly sliced
- 150 g Red Cabbage, thinly sliced
- 1 Apple (about 150 g), julienned
- 50 g Carrot, grated
- 30 ml Apple Cider Vinegar
- 15 ml Olive Oil
- 10 g Honey
- 5 g Dijon Mustard
- 2 g Salt
- 1 g Black Pepper
- 10 g Fresh Parsley, chopped

Directions

1. In a large mixing bowl, combine the green cabbage, red cabbage, apple, and carrot.
2. In a separate small bowl, whisk together the apple cider vinegar, olive oil, honey, Dijon mustard, salt, and black pepper until well combined.
3. Pour the dressing over the cabbage mixture and toss until everything is evenly coated.
4. Sprinkle the chopped parsley over the slaw and gently mix to incorporate.
5. Let the slaw sit for at least 10 minutes before serving to allow the flavors to meld.

Nutritional Information

Calories: 120, Protein: 2g, Carbohydrates: 18g, Fat: 5g, Fiber: 4g, Cholesterol: 0 mg, Salt: 200 mg, Potassium: 300 mg

WHOLE-WHEAT COUSCOUS WITH NUTS AND RAISINS

Servings 4 | Prep: 10 min | Cook: 10 min

This delightful dish combines the nutty flavor of whole-wheat couscous with the sweetness of raisins and the crunch of nuts, creating a heart-healthy side that's both satisfying and nutritious.

Equipment

Medium Saucepan, Mixing Bowl, Fork

Ingredients

- 200 g Whole-Wheat Couscous
- 300 ml Low-Sodium Vegetable Broth
- 50 g Raisins
- 50 g Almonds, chopped
- 50 g Walnuts, chopped
- 10 ml Olive Oil
- 5 g Fresh Parsley, chopped
- 2 g Ground Cinnamon
- Salt, to taste

Directions

1. In a medium saucepan, bring the vegetable broth to a boil.
2. Stir in the whole-wheat couscous, cover, and remove from heat. Let it sit for 5 minutes.
3. Fluff the couscous with a fork and transfer it to a mixing bowl.
4. Add the raisins, almonds, walnuts, olive oil, parsley, and cinnamon to the couscous.
5. Mix well and season with salt to taste. Serve warm or at room temperature.

Nutritional Information

Calories: 320, Protein: 8g, Carbohydrates: 45g, Fat: 13g, Fiber: 7g, Cholesterol: 0 mg, Salt: 120 mg, Potassium: 280 mg

GREEN BEAN SALAD WITH ALMONDS

Servings 4 | Prep: 10 min | Cook: 5 min

This vibrant salad combines crisp green beans with the nutty crunch of almonds, offering a refreshing and heart-healthy side dish perfect for any meal.

Equipment

Medium Pot, Large Bowl, Skillet

Ingredients

- 400 g Green Beans, trimmed
- 50 g Almonds, sliced
- 30 ml Olive Oil
- 15 ml Lemon Juice
- 1 clove Garlic, minced
- 5 g Fresh Parsley, chopped
- Salt and Pepper to taste

Directions

1. Bring a medium pot of water to a boil. Add green beans and cook for 3-4 minutes until tender-crisp. Drain and rinse under cold water.
2. In a skillet, toast the almonds over medium heat until golden brown, about 2-3 minutes. Set aside.
3. In a large bowl, whisk together olive oil, lemon juice, and minced garlic.
4. Add the green beans to the bowl and toss to coat with the dressing.
5. Sprinkle with toasted almonds and chopped parsley. Season with salt and pepper to taste.

Nutritional Information

Calories: 150, Protein: 4g, Carbohydrates: 10g, Fat: 11g, Fiber: 4g, Cholesterol: 0 mg, Salt: 50 mg, Potassium: 250 mg

BALSAMIC MUSHROOMS WITH GARLIC

Servings 4 | Prep: 10 min | Cook: 15 min

Savor the rich, earthy flavors of mushrooms enhanced by a tangy balsamic glaze and aromatic garlic. This dish is a perfect heart-healthy side that complements any meal.

Equipment

Large Skillet, Wooden Spoon, Measuring Cups and Spoons

Ingredients

- 500 g Button Mushrooms, cleaned and halved
- 30 ml Olive Oil
- 3 cloves Garlic, minced
- 60 ml Balsamic Vinegar
- 5 g Fresh Thyme Leaves
- Salt and Pepper to taste

Directions

1. Heat olive oil in a large skillet over medium heat.
2. Add the minced garlic and sauté for 1-2 minutes until fragrant.
3. Add the mushrooms to the skillet, stirring occasionally, and cook for about 5 minutes until they start to brown.
4. Pour in the balsamic vinegar and add fresh thyme leaves. Stir well to coat the mushrooms.
5. Cook for an additional 5-8 minutes until the mushrooms are tender and the balsamic vinegar has reduced to a glaze.
6. Season with salt and pepper to taste before serving.

Nutritional Information

Calories: 110, Protein: 3g, Carbohydrates: 9g, Fat: 7g, Fiber: 2g, Cholesterol: 0 mg, Salt: 10 mg, Potassium: 400 mg

SWEET CORN AND AVOCADO SALAD

Servings 4 | Prep: 15 min | Cook: 0 min

A refreshing and vibrant salad that combines the sweetness of corn with the creaminess of avocado, perfect for a heart-healthy meal.

Equipment

Mixing Bowl, Knife, Cutting Board

Ingredients

- 300 g Sweet Corn (cooked and cooled)
- 2 Avocados (ripe, diced)
- 150 g Cherry Tomatoes (halved)
- 50 g Red Onion (finely chopped)
- 30 ml Lime Juice (freshly squeezed)
- 15 ml Olive Oil
- 10 g Fresh Cilantro (chopped)
- Salt and Pepper to taste

Directions

1. In a mixing bowl, combine the sweet corn, diced avocados, cherry tomatoes, and red onion.
2. Drizzle the lime juice and olive oil over the salad mixture.
3. Gently toss the ingredients to ensure even coating and distribution.
4. Add the chopped cilantro and season with salt and pepper to taste.
5. Serve immediately or chill for 10 minutes for enhanced flavors.

Nutritional Information

Calories: 220, Protein: 4g, Carbohydrates: 25g, Fat: 14g, Fiber: 7g, Cholesterol: 0 mg, Salt: 150 mg, Potassium: 600 mg

BUTTERNUT SQUASH AND QUINOA SIDE

Servings 4 | Prep: 15 min | Cook: 25 min

This vibrant and nutritious side dish combines the nutty flavor of quinoa with the sweet, earthy taste of roasted butternut squash, making it a perfect heart-healthy addition to any meal.

Equipment

Baking Sheet, Medium Saucepan, Mixing Bowl

Ingredients

- 500 g Butternut Squash, peeled and cubed
- 200 g Quinoa
- 30 ml Olive Oil
- 5 g Ground Cumin
- 2 g Salt
- 500 ml Water
- 50 g Chopped Fresh Parsley
- 30 ml Lemon Juice

Directions

1. Preheat the oven to 200°C.
2. Toss the butternut squash cubes with olive oil, cumin, and salt. Spread evenly on a baking sheet and roast for 20 minutes until tender.
3. Rinse quinoa under cold water. In a medium saucepan, bring water to a boil, add quinoa, reduce heat, cover, and simmer for 15 minutes until water is absorbed.
4. In a mixing bowl, combine roasted squash, cooked quinoa, parsley, and lemon juice.
5. Toss gently to mix all ingredients well. Serve warm or at room temperature.

Nutritional Information

Calories: 280, Protein: 7g, Carbohydrates: 45g, Fat: 9g, Fiber: 7g, Cholesterol: 0 mg, Salt: 500 mg, Potassium: 700 mg

Soups and Stews

LENTIL AND SPINACH SOUP

Servings 4 | Prep: 15 min | Cook: 30 min

This hearty and nutritious soup combines the earthy flavors of lentils with the freshness of spinach, making it a perfect heart-healthy meal.

Equipment

Large Pot, Wooden Spoon, Measuring Cups

Ingredients

- 200 g Lentils
- 1 l Vegetable Broth
- 150 g Fresh Spinach
- 1 Medium Onion, chopped
- 2 Cloves Garlic, minced
- 2 Medium Carrots, diced
- 2 Stalks Celery, diced
- 15 ml Olive Oil
- 5 g Ground Cumin
- 5 g Ground Coriander
- Salt and Pepper to taste

Directions

1. Heat olive oil in a large pot over medium heat. Add onion, garlic, carrots, and celery; sauté until softened.
2. Stir in cumin and coriander, cooking for an additional minute until fragrant.
3. Add lentils and vegetable broth to the pot. Bring to a boil, then reduce heat and simmer for 20 minutes.
4. Stir in spinach and cook for another 5 minutes until wilted.
5. Season with salt and pepper to taste. Serve hot.

Nutritional Information

Calories: 250, Protein: 12g, Carbohydrates: 40g, Fat: 5g, Fiber: 15g, Cholesterol: 0 mg, Salt: 400 mg, Potassium: 600 mg

TOMATO AND WHITE BEAN SOUP

Servings 4 | Prep: 15 min | Cook: 30 min

This hearty and flavorful soup combines the richness of tomatoes with the creaminess of white beans, offering a comforting and nutritious meal perfect for heart health.

Equipment

Large Pot, Blender or Immersion Blender, Ladle

Ingredients

- 15 ml olive oil
- 1 onion, chopped (about 150 g)
- 2 cloves garlic, minced
- 400 g canned tomatoes, crushed
- 500 ml low-sodium vegetable broth
- 240 g canned white beans, drained and rinsed
- 5 g dried basil
- 5 g dried oregano
- Salt and pepper to taste

Directions

1. Heat olive oil in a large pot over medium heat. Add the chopped onion and garlic, sautéing until the onion is translucent.
2. Stir in the crushed tomatoes and cook for 5 minutes, allowing the flavors to meld.
3. Add the vegetable broth, white beans, basil, and oregano. Bring the mixture to a boil, then reduce the heat and simmer for 20 minutes.
4. Use a blender or immersion blender to puree the soup until smooth, or leave it slightly chunky if preferred.
5. Season with salt and pepper to taste, then ladle into bowls and serve warm.

Nutritional Information

Calories: 180, Protein: 7g, Carbohydrates: 30g, Fat: 4g, Fiber: 8g, Cholesterol: 0 mg, Salt: 150 mg, Potassium: 600 mg

BUTTERNUT SQUASH AND GINGER SOUP

Servings 4 | Prep: 15 min | Cook: 30 min

This velvety butternut squash and ginger soup is a comforting, heart-healthy choice, perfect for warming up on a chilly day. The ginger adds a zesty kick, while the squash provides a creamy texture without the need for cream.

Equipment

Large pot, Blender or immersion blender, Knife and cutting board

Ingredients

- 1 kg butternut squash, peeled and cubed
- 1 medium onion, chopped
- 15 g fresh ginger, grated
- 2 cloves garlic, minced
- 1 liter low-sodium vegetable broth
- 15 ml olive oil
- 5 g ground cumin
- Salt and pepper to taste
- 10 g fresh parsley, chopped (for garnish)

Directions

1. Heat olive oil in a large pot over medium heat. Add onion, garlic, and ginger, sauté until onion is translucent.
2. Add cubed butternut squash and ground cumin, stirring to coat the squash with the spices.
3. Pour in the vegetable broth, bring to a boil, then reduce heat and simmer for 20 minutes, or until squash is tender.
4. Remove from heat and blend the soup until smooth using a blender or immersion blender.
5. Season with salt and pepper to taste, then serve hot, garnished with fresh parsley.

Nutritional Information

Calories: 180, Protein: 3g, Carbohydrates: 35g, Fat: 5g, Fiber: 6g, Cholesterol: 0 mg, Salt: 150 mg, Potassium: 600 mg

HEARTY VEGETABLE BARLEY SOUP

Servings 6 | Prep: 15 min | Cook: 45 min

This nourishing soup combines wholesome vegetables and hearty barley, making it a perfect choice for a heart-healthy meal. It's both comforting and satisfying, ideal for any season.

Equipment

Large Pot, Wooden Spoon, Knife

Ingredients

- 200 g pearl barley
- 1 l low-sodium vegetable broth
- 2 carrots, diced (about 150 g)
- 2 celery stalks, diced (about 100 g)
- 1 onion, chopped (about 150 g)
- 2 cloves garlic, minced
- 400 g canned tomatoes, chopped
- 1 zucchini, diced (about 150 g)
- 1 tsp dried thyme
- 1 tsp dried basil
- Salt and pepper to taste
- 10 ml olive oil

Directions

1. Heat olive oil in a large pot over medium heat. Add onion and garlic, sauté until fragrant.
2. Stir in carrots and celery, cooking for about 5 minutes until slightly softened.
3. Add barley, canned tomatoes, and vegetable broth. Bring to a boil.
4. Reduce heat, cover, and simmer for 30 minutes.
5. Add zucchini, thyme, and basil. Continue to simmer for another 10 minutes until barley is tender.
6. Season with salt and pepper to taste. Serve hot.

Nutritional Information

Calories: 180, Protein: 5g, Carbohydrates: 35g, Fat: 3g, Fiber: 8g, Cholesterol: 0 mg, Salt: 150 mg, Potassium: 500 mg

MEDITERRANEAN MINESTRONE

Servings 6 | Prep: 15 min | Cook: 30 min

This Mediterranean Minestrone is a heart-healthy, vibrant soup filled with colorful vegetables and aromatic herbs, perfect for a nourishing meal.

Equipment

Large Pot, Cutting Board, Knife

Ingredients

- 15 ml Olive Oil
- 1 Onion, chopped (about 150 g)
- 2 Garlic Cloves, minced
- 1 Zucchini, diced (about 200 g)
- 1 Red Bell Pepper, diced (about 150 g)
- 400 g Canned Diced Tomatoes
- 1.5 l Low-Sodium Vegetable Broth
- 100 g Whole Wheat Pasta
- 200 g Canned Cannellini Beans, drained and rinsed
- 100 g Spinach Leaves
- 5 g Dried Oregano
- 5 g Dried Basil
- Salt and Pepper to taste

Directions

1. Heat olive oil in a large pot over medium heat. Add onion and garlic, sauté until onion is translucent.
2. Stir in zucchini and red bell pepper, cooking until slightly softened.
3. Add canned tomatoes, vegetable broth, oregano, and basil. Bring to a boil.
4. Stir in pasta and beans, reduce heat, and simmer until pasta is al dente.
5. Add spinach, cooking until wilted. Season with salt and pepper to taste.

Nutritional Information

Calories: 220, Protein: 8g, Carbohydrates: 38g, Fat: 5g, Fiber: 8g, Cholesterol: 0 mg, Salt: 150 mg, Potassium: 600 mg

CAULIFLOWER AND LEEK SOUP

Servings 4 | Prep: 15 min | Cook: 30 min

This creamy cauliflower and leek soup is a comforting, heart-healthy dish that is both flavorful and nourishing. Perfect for a cozy meal, it combines the subtle sweetness of leeks with the mild, nutty flavor of cauliflower.

Equipment

Large Pot, Blender, Knife

Ingredients

- 500 g Cauliflower, chopped
- 200 g Leeks, sliced
- 1 L Low-sodium vegetable broth
- 15 ml Olive oil
- 2 cloves Garlic, minced
- 5 g Fresh thyme leaves
- 2 g Black pepper
- 2 g Salt

Directions

1. Heat olive oil in a large pot over medium heat. Add leeks and garlic, sauté until soft.
2. Add cauliflower and thyme, stirring for 2 minutes.
3. Pour in the vegetable broth, bring to a boil, then reduce heat and simmer for 20 minutes.
4. Blend the soup until smooth using a blender.
5. Season with salt and pepper to taste, then serve warm.

Nutritional Information

Calories: 120, Protein: 5g, Carbohydrates: 18g, Fat: 4g, Fiber: 5g, Cholesterol: 0 mg, Salt: 300 mg, Potassium: 450 mg

BLACK BEAN AND SWEET POTATO STEW

Servings 4 | Prep: 15 min | Cook: 30 min

This hearty and nutritious stew combines the richness of black beans with the natural sweetness of sweet potatoes, creating a comforting dish perfect for heart health.

Equipment

Large Pot, Wooden Spoon, Knife

Ingredients

- 400 g Black Beans (canned, drained, and rinsed)
- 500 g Sweet Potatoes (peeled and diced)
- 1 Onion (150 g, chopped)
- 2 Garlic Cloves (minced)
- 1 Red Bell Pepper (150 g, chopped)
- 800 ml Vegetable Broth
- 1 tsp Ground Cumin
- 1 tsp Smoked Paprika
- 1 tbsp Olive Oil
- Salt and Pepper to taste

Directions

1. Heat olive oil in a large pot over medium heat. Add onion and garlic, sauté until onion is translucent.
2. Stir in red bell pepper, sweet potatoes, cumin, and smoked paprika. Cook for 5 minutes.
3. Add black beans and vegetable broth. Bring to a boil, then reduce heat and simmer for 20 minutes, or until sweet potatoes are tender.
4. Season with salt and pepper to taste.
5. Serve hot, garnished with fresh herbs if desired.

Nutritional Information

Calories: 320, Protein: 10g, Carbohydrates: 60g, Fat: 6g, Fiber: 14g, Cholesterol: 0 mg, Salt: 480 mg, Potassium: 950 mg

CREAMY CARROT AND TURMERIC SOUP

Servings 4 | Prep: 15 min | Cook: 25 min

This vibrant and creamy carrot and turmeric soup is both nourishing and flavorful, offering a perfect blend of spices and creaminess without the use of dairy.

Equipment

Large Pot, Blender, Ladle

Ingredients

- 500 g carrots, peeled and chopped
- 1 medium onion, chopped
- 2 cloves garlic, minced
- 15 ml olive oil
- 1 tsp ground turmeric
- 1 liter low-sodium vegetable broth
- 200 ml coconut milk
- Salt and pepper to taste
- Fresh coriander for garnish

Directions

1. Heat olive oil in a large pot over medium heat. Add onions and garlic, sauté until onions are translucent.
2. Stir in turmeric and cook for an additional minute until fragrant.
3. Add carrots and vegetable broth. Bring to a boil, then reduce heat and simmer until carrots are tender, about 20 minutes.
4. Remove from heat and blend the soup until smooth using a blender.
5. Return the soup to the pot, stir in coconut milk, and season with salt and pepper. Heat gently until warmed through.
6. Serve hot, garnished with fresh coriander.

Nutritional Information

Calories: 180, Protein: 3g, Carbohydrates: 20g, Fat: 10g, Fiber: 5g, Cholesterol: 0 mg, Salt: 200 mg, Potassium: 600 mg

CHICKPEA AND KALE STEW

Servings 4 | Prep: 15 min | Cook: 30 min

This hearty and nutritious stew combines the earthy flavors of chickpeas and kale, offering a comforting dish that's perfect for maintaining heart health.

Equipment

Large Pot, Wooden Spoon, Knife

Ingredients

- 15 ml Olive Oil
- 1 Onion, chopped (about 150 g)
- 2 Garlic Cloves, minced
- 400 g Canned Chickpeas, drained and rinsed
- 500 ml Low-Sodium Vegetable Broth
- 200 g Kale, chopped
- 1 Tomato, diced (about 150 g)
- 5 g Ground Cumin
- 5 g Paprika
- Salt and Pepper to taste

Directions

1. Heat olive oil in a large pot over medium heat. Add onion and garlic, sauté until onion is translucent.
2. Stir in chickpeas, vegetable broth, and diced tomato. Bring to a simmer.
3. Add kale, cumin, and paprika. Stir well and let simmer for 20 minutes.
4. Season with salt and pepper to taste. Adjust seasoning as needed.
5. Serve hot, garnished with fresh herbs if desired.

Nutritional Information

Calories: 220, Protein: 9g, Carbohydrates: 35g, Fat: 6g, Fiber: 10g, Cholesterol: 0 mg, Salt: 150 mg, Potassium: 600 mg

MUSHROOM AND WILD RICE SOUP

Servings 4 | Prep: 15 min | Cook: 45 min

This hearty and earthy soup combines the rich flavors of mushrooms with the nutty texture of wild rice, creating a comforting and nourishing dish perfect for heart health.

Equipment

Large Pot, Cutting Board, Knife

Ingredients

- 200 g Mushrooms, sliced
- 100 g Wild Rice
- 1 L Vegetable Broth
- 1 Onion, chopped
- 2 Cloves Garlic, minced
- 1 Carrot, diced
- 1 Celery Stalk, diced
- 15 ml Olive Oil
- 5 g Fresh Thyme
- Salt and Pepper to taste

Directions

1. Heat olive oil in a large pot over medium heat. Add onions, garlic, carrots, and celery, sautéing until softened.
2. Stir in the mushrooms and cook until they release their moisture and begin to brown.
3. Add the wild rice, vegetable broth, and thyme. Bring to a boil.
4. Reduce heat to low, cover, and simmer for 40 minutes, or until the rice is tender.
5. Season with salt and pepper to taste before serving.

Nutritional Information

Calories: 180, Protein: 6g, Carbohydrates: 30g, Fat: 5g, Fiber: 4g, Cholesterol: 0 mg, Salt: 400 mg, Potassium: 450 mg

SPICED PUMPKIN SOUP

Servings 4 | Prep: 15 min | Cook: 30 min

This Spiced Pumpkin Soup is a warm, comforting dish perfect for heart health. It combines the earthy sweetness of pumpkin with aromatic spices, creating a nourishing and flavorful experience.

Equipment

Large Pot, Blender or Immersion Blender, Ladle

Ingredients

- 800 g pumpkin, peeled and cubed
- 1 medium onion, chopped
- 2 cloves garlic, minced
- 15 ml olive oil
- 1 liter low-sodium vegetable broth
- 5 g ground cumin
- 5 g ground coriander
- 2 g ground cinnamon
- 2 g ground nutmeg
- 100 ml low-fat coconut milk
- Salt and pepper to taste

Directions

1. Heat olive oil in a large pot over medium heat. Add onion and garlic, sauté until soft.
2. Stir in cumin, coriander, cinnamon, and nutmeg, cooking for 1 minute until fragrant.
3. Add pumpkin cubes and vegetable broth. Bring to a boil, then reduce heat and simmer for 20 minutes, or until pumpkin is tender.
4. Use a blender or immersion blender to puree the soup until smooth.
5. Stir in coconut milk, season with salt and pepper, and heat through.

Nutritional Information

Calories: 180, Protein: 3g, Carbohydrates: 28g, Fat: 7g, Fiber: 5g, Cholesterol: 0 mg, Salt: 150 mg, Potassium: 600 mg

LEMON AND DILL CHICKEN SOUP

Servings 4 | Prep: 15 min | Cook: 30 min

This refreshing and aromatic soup combines the zesty flavor of lemon with the earthy aroma of dill, creating a heart-healthy dish that's both comforting and invigorating.

Equipment

Large Pot, Cutting Board, Knife

Ingredients

- 500 g Chicken Breast, diced
- 1 l Low-Sodium Chicken Broth
- 200 g Carrots, sliced
- 150 g Celery, chopped
- 100 g Onion, diced
- 2 cloves Garlic, minced
- 1 Lemon, juiced
- 10 g Fresh Dill, chopped
- 30 ml Olive Oil
- Salt and Pepper to taste

Directions

1. Heat olive oil in a large pot over medium heat. Add onion, garlic, carrots, and celery, sautéing until softened.
2. Add diced chicken breast to the pot, cooking until lightly browned.
3. Pour in the chicken broth and bring to a boil. Reduce heat and let simmer for 20 minutes.
4. Stir in lemon juice and fresh dill, seasoning with salt and pepper to taste.
5. Simmer for an additional 5 minutes, then serve hot.

Nutritional Information

Calories: 250, Protein: 30g, Carbohydrates: 15g, Fat: 8g, Fiber: 3g, Cholesterol: 60 mg, Salt: 300 mg, Potassium: 600 mg

QUINOA AND RED LENTIL SOUP

Servings 4 | Prep: 10 min | Cook: 30 min

This hearty and nutritious soup combines the protein-rich goodness of quinoa and red lentils, offering a comforting and satisfying meal that's perfect for heart health.

Equipment

Large Pot, Wooden Spoon, Measuring Cups and Spoons

Ingredients

- 100 g quinoa
- 150 g red lentils
- 1 l vegetable broth
- 1 onion, chopped
- 2 carrots, diced
- 2 celery stalks, diced
- 2 garlic cloves, minced
- 5 ml olive oil
- 5 g ground cumin
- 5 g ground coriander
- 5 g turmeric
- Salt and pepper to taste
- 10 g fresh parsley, chopped (for garnish)

Directions

1. Rinse quinoa and red lentils under cold water until the water runs clear.
2. In a large pot, heat olive oil over medium heat. Add onion, carrots, celery, and garlic; sauté until vegetables are softened.
3. Stir in cumin, coriander, and turmeric, cooking for an additional minute until fragrant.
4. Add quinoa, red lentils, and vegetable broth to the pot. Bring to a boil, then reduce heat and simmer for 20-25 minutes, or until quinoa and lentils are tender.
5. Season with salt and pepper to taste. Serve hot, garnished with fresh parsley.

Nutritional Information

Calories: 250, Protein: 12g, Carbohydrates: 45g, Fat: 4g, Fiber: 10g, Cholesterol: 0 mg, Salt: 300 mg, Potassium: 600 mg

ROASTED GARLIC AND TOMATO SOUP

Servings 4 | Prep: 15 min | Cook: 45 min

This comforting soup combines the rich flavors of roasted garlic and tomatoes, creating a heart-healthy dish that's both delicious and nourishing.

Equipment

Oven, Blender, Saucepan

Ingredients

- 800 g ripe tomatoes, halved
- 1 bulb garlic, top trimmed
- 15 ml olive oil
- 500 ml low-sodium vegetable broth
- 5 g fresh basil leaves
- 5 g salt
- 2 g black pepper

Directions

1. Preheat the oven to 200°C. Place the tomatoes and garlic bulb on a baking sheet. Drizzle with olive oil and roast for 30 minutes.
2. Once roasted, allow the garlic to cool slightly, then squeeze the cloves out of their skins.
3. In a blender, combine the roasted tomatoes, garlic, and vegetable broth. Blend until smooth.
4. Transfer the mixture to a saucepan and bring to a simmer over medium heat.
5. Stir in the basil, salt, and pepper. Simmer for 10 minutes to let the flavors meld.
6. Serve hot, garnished with additional basil if desired.

Nutritional Information

Calories: 120, Protein: 3g, Carbohydrates: 18g, Fat: 5g, Fiber: 4g, Cholesterol: 0 mg, Salt: 300 mg, Potassium: 600 mg

SPICY MOROCCAN CHICKPEA SOUP

Servings 4 | Prep: 15 min | Cook: 30 min

This vibrant and aromatic soup combines the warmth of Moroccan spices with the heartiness of chickpeas, creating a nourishing and flavorful dish perfect for any season.

Equipment

Large Pot, Wooden Spoon, Measuring Cups and Spoons

Ingredients

- 15 ml olive oil
- 1 medium onion, chopped (about 150 g)
- 2 cloves garlic, minced
- 5 g ground cumin
- 5 g ground coriander
- 2 g smoked paprika
- 1 g cayenne pepper
- 400 g canned chickpeas, drained and rinsed
- 400 g canned tomatoes, chopped
- 750 ml vegetable broth
- 100 g carrots, diced
- 1 g salt
- 2 g black pepper
- 30 g fresh cilantro, chopped (for garnish)

Directions

1. Heat olive oil in a large pot over medium heat. Add onion and garlic, sauté until soft.
2. Stir in cumin, coriander, smoked paprika, and cayenne pepper, cooking for 1 minute until fragrant.
3. Add chickpeas, tomatoes, vegetable broth, and carrots. Season with salt and pepper.
4. Bring to a boil, then reduce heat and simmer for 20 minutes, allowing flavors to meld.
5. Adjust seasoning if necessary. Serve hot, garnished with fresh cilantro.

Nutritional Information

Calories: 220, Protein: 8g, Carbohydrates: 35g, Fat: 6g, Fiber: 10g, Cholesterol: 0 mg, Salt: 400 mg, Potassium: 600 mg

GREEN PEA AND MINT SOUP

Servings 4 | Prep: 10 min | Cook: 20 min

This refreshing and vibrant soup combines the sweetness of peas with the coolness of mint, creating a heart-healthy dish that's both nourishing and delicious.

Equipment

Medium Pot, Blender, Ladle

Ingredients

- 500 g fresh or frozen green peas
- 1 medium onion, chopped (approximately 150 g)
- 1 tablespoon olive oil (approximately 15 ml)
- 750 ml low-sodium vegetable broth
- 10 g fresh mint leaves
- 1 teaspoon lemon juice (approximately 5 ml)
- Salt and pepper to taste

Directions

1. Heat the olive oil in a medium pot over medium heat. Add the chopped onion and sauté until translucent, about 5 minutes.
2. Add the green peas and vegetable broth to the pot. Bring to a boil, then reduce the heat and simmer for 10 minutes.
3. Remove the pot from heat and add the fresh mint leaves.
4. Using a blender, carefully blend the soup until smooth.
5. Stir in the lemon juice and season with salt and pepper to taste.
6. Serve hot, garnished with additional mint leaves if desired.

Nutritional Information

Calories: 180, Protein: 8g, Carbohydrates: 28g, Fat: 5g, Fiber: 8g, Cholesterol: 0 mg, Salt: 150 mg, Potassium: 400 mg

MISO SOUP WITH TOFU AND SEAWEED

Servings 4 | Prep: 10 min | Cook: 10 min

A delicate and nourishing soup, Miso Soup with Tofu and Seaweed is a heart-healthy choice that combines the umami flavors of miso with the freshness of tofu and seaweed.

Equipment

Medium Saucepan, Ladle, Mixing Spoon

Ingredients

- 1 liter water
- 50 g miso paste
- 200 g firm tofu, cubed
- 10 g dried wakame seaweed
- 50 g green onions, sliced
- 15 ml low-sodium soy sauce

Directions

1. In a medium saucepan, bring the water to a gentle simmer over medium heat.
2. Add the miso paste, stirring until fully dissolved.
3. Incorporate the tofu cubes and dried wakame seaweed, allowing them to simmer for 5 minutes.
4. Stir in the sliced green onions and soy sauce, cooking for an additional 2 minutes.
5. Serve hot, garnished with extra green onions if desired.

Nutritional Information

Calories: 80, Protein: 6g, Carbohydrates: 8g, Fat: 3g, Fiber: 1g, Cholesterol: 0mg, Salt: 300mg, Potassium: 150mg

BROCCOLI AND ALMOND SOUP

Servings 4 | Prep: 10 min | Cook: 20 min

This creamy broccoli and almond soup is a heart-healthy delight, combining the earthy flavors of broccoli with the nutty richness of almonds for a comforting and nutritious meal.

Equipment

Blender, Saucepan, Knife

Ingredients

- 500 g broccoli, chopped
- 1 onion, chopped
- 2 cloves garlic, minced
- 750 ml low-sodium vegetable broth
- 50 g almonds, blanched
- 15 ml olive oil
- 5 g salt
- 2 g black pepper
- 10 ml lemon juice

Directions

1. Heat olive oil in a saucepan over medium heat. Add onion and garlic, sauté until soft.
2. Add broccoli and almonds, cook for 5 minutes, stirring occasionally.
3. Pour in vegetable broth, bring to a boil, then reduce heat and simmer for 15 minutes.
4. Blend the mixture until smooth using a blender.
5. Return to saucepan, add salt, pepper, and lemon juice, and heat through before serving.

Nutritional Information

Calories: 180, Protein: 7g, Carbohydrates: 15g, Fat: 11g, Fiber: 6g, Cholesterol: 0 mg, Salt: 300 mg, Potassium: 450 mg

SLOW-COOKED TOMATO BASIL SOUP

Servings 6 | Prep: 15 min | Cook: 240 min

This comforting and heart-healthy tomato basil soup is slow-cooked to perfection, allowing the flavors to meld beautifully. It's a nourishing choice for a cozy meal.

Equipment

Slow Cooker, Blender, Knife

Ingredients

- 1 kg ripe tomatoes, chopped
- 200 g carrots, diced
- 150 g onions, chopped
- 4 cloves garlic, minced
- 500 ml low-sodium vegetable broth
- 15 g fresh basil leaves, chopped
- 10 ml olive oil
- 5 g salt
- 2 g black pepper

Directions

1. Heat olive oil in a pan and sauté onions, garlic, and carrots until softened.
2. Transfer the sautéed vegetables to the slow cooker.
3. Add chopped tomatoes, vegetable broth, salt, and pepper to the slow cooker.
4. Cover and cook on low for 4 hours until vegetables are tender.
5. Blend the soup until smooth using a blender.
6. Stir in fresh basil and adjust seasoning if necessary.
7. Serve warm, garnished with additional basil if desired.

Nutritional Information

Calories: 120, Protein: 3g, Carbohydrates: 22g, Fat: 3g, Fiber: 5g, Cholesterol: 0 mg, Salt: 200 mg, Potassium: 650 mg

ZUCCHINI AND SPINACH SOUP

Servings 4 | Prep: 10 min | Cook: 20 min

This vibrant and nourishing soup combines the delicate flavors of zucchini and spinach, creating a heart-healthy dish that's both comforting and refreshing.

Equipment

Large Pot, Blender, Ladle

Ingredients

- 500 g zucchini, sliced
- 200 g fresh spinach leaves
- 1 medium onion, chopped
- 2 cloves garlic, minced
- 1 liter low-sodium vegetable broth
- 15 ml olive oil
- Salt and pepper to taste

Directions

1. Heat olive oil in a large pot over medium heat. Add onion and garlic, sauté until translucent.
2. Add zucchini slices and cook for 5 minutes, stirring occasionally.
3. Pour in the vegetable broth, bring to a boil, then reduce heat and simmer for 10 minutes.
4. Add spinach leaves and cook until wilted, about 2 minutes.
5. Use a blender to puree the soup until smooth. Season with salt and pepper to taste.
6. Serve hot, garnished with a sprinkle of fresh herbs if desired.

Nutritional Information

Calories: 120, Protein: 4g, Carbohydrates: 18g, Fat: 4g, Fiber: 4g, Cholesterol: 0 mg, Salt: 150 mg, Potassium: 650 mg

RED CABBAGE AND APPLE SOUP

Servings 4 | Prep: 15 min | Cook: 30 min

This vibrant and tangy soup combines the natural sweetness of apples with the earthy flavors of red cabbage, creating a heart-healthy dish that's both nourishing and delicious.

Equipment

Large Pot, Blender, Knife

Ingredients

- 500 g Red Cabbage, shredded
- 2 Apples, peeled and chopped
- 1 Onion, chopped
- 2 cloves Garlic, minced
- 1 l Low-sodium Vegetable Broth
- 15 ml Olive Oil
- 5 g Fresh Thyme, chopped
- 5 g Black Pepper
- 2 g Salt

Directions

1. Heat olive oil in a large pot over medium heat. Add onion and garlic, sauté until translucent.
2. Add shredded red cabbage and chopped apples to the pot, stirring to combine.
3. Pour in the vegetable broth, then add thyme, salt, and pepper. Bring to a boil.
4. Reduce heat and simmer for 20 minutes, until cabbage is tender.
5. Use a blender to puree the soup until smooth. Adjust seasoning if necessary.
6. Serve hot, garnished with a sprinkle of fresh thyme.

Nutritional Information

Calories: 120, Protein: 3g, Carbohydrates: 25g, Fat: 3g, Fiber: 6g, Cholesterol: 0 mg, Salt: 200 mg, Potassium: 400 mg

GINGERED CARROT AND COCONUT SOUP

Servings 4 | Prep: 15 min | Cook: 25 min

This vibrant and creamy soup combines the natural sweetness of carrots with the warmth of ginger and the richness of coconut milk, creating a heart-healthy delight that's both comforting and nourishing.

Equipment

Blender, Large Pot, Knife

Ingredients

- 500 g carrots, peeled and chopped
- 1 medium onion, chopped
- 2 cloves garlic, minced
- 15 g fresh ginger, grated
- 400 ml light coconut milk
- 500 ml low-sodium vegetable broth
- 15 ml olive oil
- Salt and pepper to taste
- Fresh coriander for garnish

Directions

1. Heat olive oil in a large pot over medium heat. Add onion, garlic, and ginger, sauté until fragrant.
2. Add carrots and cook for 5 minutes, stirring occasionally.
3. Pour in vegetable broth and bring to a boil. Reduce heat and simmer until carrots are tender, about 15 minutes.
4. Stir in coconut milk, then blend the mixture until smooth using a blender.
5. Season with salt and pepper to taste. Reheat gently if necessary.
6. Serve hot, garnished with fresh coriander.

Nutritional Information

Calories: 180, Protein: 3g, Carbohydrates: 20g, Fat: 10g, Fiber: 4g, Cholesterol: 0 mg, Salt: 150 mg, Potassium: 600 mg

SWEET CORN AND ROASTED RED PEPPER SOUP

Servings 4 | Prep: 15 min | Cook: 25 min

This vibrant and creamy soup combines the natural sweetness of corn with the smoky depth of roasted red peppers, creating a comforting and heart-healthy dish.

Equipment

Blender, Large Pot, Baking Sheet

Ingredients

- 500 g sweet corn kernels (fresh or frozen)
- 2 large red peppers
- 1 medium onion, chopped
- 2 cloves garlic, minced
- 750 ml low-sodium vegetable broth
- 15 ml olive oil
- 5 g ground cumin
- Salt and pepper to taste
- 10 g fresh cilantro, chopped (optional for garnish)

Directions

1. Preheat the oven to 200°C. Place the red peppers on a baking sheet and roast for 20 minutes, turning halfway through, until the skin is charred.
2. While the peppers are roasting, heat olive oil in a large pot over medium heat. Sauté the onion and garlic until softened, about 5 minutes.
3. Add the sweet corn, ground cumin, and vegetable broth to the pot. Bring to a simmer and cook for 10 minutes.
4. Once the peppers are roasted, remove the skins, seeds, and stems. Chop the peppers and add them to the pot.
5. Use a blender to puree the soup until smooth. Return to the pot and season with salt and pepper to taste.
6. Serve hot, garnished with fresh cilantro if desired.

Nutritional Information

Calories: 180, Protein: 5g, Carbohydrates: 35g, Fat: 5g, Fiber: 6g, Cholesterol: 0 mg, Salt: 150 mg, Potassium: 450 mg

CABBAGE AND LENTIL SOUP

Servings 4 | Prep: 15 min | Cook: 40 min

This hearty and nourishing cabbage and lentil soup is perfect for a heart-healthy diet. Packed with fiber and plant-based protein, it's both satisfying and delicious.

Equipment

Large Pot, Wooden Spoon, Knife

Ingredients

- 200 g Green Lentils
- 500 g Cabbage, shredded
- 1 Onion, chopped
- 2 Carrots, diced
- 2 Garlic Cloves, minced
- 1.5 l Vegetable Broth
- 15 ml Olive Oil
- 5 g Ground Cumin
- 5 g Paprika
- Salt and Pepper to taste

Directions

1. Heat olive oil in a large pot over medium heat. Add onion, garlic, and carrots, sautéing until softened.
2. Stir in cumin and paprika, cooking for an additional minute until fragrant.
3. Add lentils, cabbage, and vegetable broth. Bring to a boil, then reduce heat and simmer for 30 minutes.
4. Season with salt and pepper to taste. Adjust seasoning as needed.
5. Serve hot, garnished with fresh herbs if desired.

Nutritional Information

Calories: 250, Protein: 12g, Carbohydrates: 40g, Fat: 5g, Fiber: 15g, Cholesterol: 0 mg, Salt: 300 mg, Potassium: 600 mg

CHILLED CUCUMBER AND AVOCADO SOUP

Servings 4 | Prep: 15 min | Cook: 0 min

This refreshing and creamy soup is perfect for a hot day. The combination of cucumber and avocado provides a smooth texture and a burst of flavor, while being heart-healthy and nutritious.

Equipment

Blender, Knife, Cutting Board

Ingredients

- 500 g cucumber, peeled and chopped
- 2 ripe avocados, peeled and pitted
- 250 ml low-fat plain yogurt
- 15 ml lime juice
- 10 g fresh dill, chopped
- 2 g salt
- 1 g black pepper
- 100 ml cold water

Directions

1. Combine cucumber, avocados, yogurt, lime juice, and dill in a blender.
2. Blend until smooth, adding cold water gradually to reach desired consistency.
3. Season with salt and black pepper to taste.
4. Chill in the refrigerator for at least 30 minutes before serving.
5. Garnish with additional dill if desired.

Nutritional Information

Calories: 180, Protein: 4g, Carbohydrates: 16g, Fat: 13g, Fiber: 7g, Cholesterol: 3mg, Salt: 200mg, Potassium: 700mg

MUSHROOM AND ONION SOUP

Servings 4 | Prep: 15 min | Cook: 30 min

This comforting Mushroom and Onion Soup is a heart-healthy delight, combining the earthy flavors of mushrooms with the sweetness of caramelized onions. Perfect for a cozy meal.

Equipment

Large Pot, Cutting Board, Knife

Ingredients

- 500 g Mushrooms, sliced
- 200 g Onions, thinly sliced
- 2 cloves Garlic, minced
- 1 l Low-sodium Vegetable Broth
- 15 ml Olive Oil
- 5 g Fresh Thyme, chopped
- 2 g Black Pepper
- 2 g Salt

Directions

1. Heat olive oil in a large pot over medium heat. Add onions and cook until caramelized, about 10 minutes.
2. Add garlic and mushrooms to the pot, sauté for another 5 minutes until mushrooms are tender.
3. Pour in the vegetable broth, then add thyme, salt, and pepper. Stir well.
4. Bring the soup to a boil, then reduce heat and let it simmer for 15 minutes.
5. Adjust seasoning if necessary and serve hot.

Nutritional Information

Calories: 120, Protein: 5g, Carbohydrates: 18g, Fat: 4g, Fiber: 3g, Cholesterol: 0 mg, Salt: 150 mg, Potassium: 450 mg

Poultry

LEMON GARLIC CHICKEN BREAST

Servings 4 | Prep: 10 min | Cook: 20 min

This Lemon Garlic Chicken Breast is a zesty and flavorful dish, perfect for a heart-healthy meal. The combination of lemon and garlic infuses the chicken with a refreshing taste, while keeping it juicy and tender.

Equipment

Skillet, Mixing Bowl, Tongs

Ingredients

- 500 g chicken breast, boneless and skinless
- 30 ml olive oil
- 3 cloves garlic, minced
- 1 lemon, juiced and zested
- 5 g dried oregano
- 2 g salt
- 2 g black pepper
- 10 g fresh parsley, chopped

Directions

1. In a mixing bowl, combine olive oil, minced garlic, lemon juice, lemon zest, dried oregano, salt, and black pepper.
2. Add the chicken breasts to the bowl, ensuring they are well coated with the marinade. Let them marinate for at least 10 minutes.
3. Heat a skillet over medium heat. Add the marinated chicken breasts and cook for about 10 minutes on each side, or until fully cooked and golden brown.
4. Remove the chicken from the skillet and let it rest for a few minutes.
5. Garnish with fresh parsley before serving.

Nutritional Information

Calories: 250, Protein: 30g, Carbohydrates: 2g, Fat: 14g, Fiber: 1g, Cholesterol: 75 mg, Salt: 500 mg, Potassium: 450 mg

BALSAMIC GRILLED CHICKEN WITH VEGGIES

Servings 4 | Prep: 15 min | Cook: 20 min

This dish combines the tangy sweetness of balsamic vinegar with juicy grilled chicken and a medley of colorful vegetables, making it a heart-healthy delight.

Equipment

Grill pan, Mixing bowl, Tongs

Ingredients

- 500 g Chicken breast, boneless and skinless
- 100 ml Balsamic vinegar
- 2 cloves Garlic, minced
- 1 tbsp Olive oil
- 200 g Bell peppers, sliced
- 150 g Zucchini, sliced
- 100 g Cherry tomatoes, halved
- 1 tsp Dried oregano
- Salt and pepper to taste

Directions

1. In a mixing bowl, combine balsamic vinegar, minced garlic, olive oil, oregano, salt, and pepper. Add chicken breasts and marinate for at least 15 minutes.
2. Preheat the grill pan over medium heat. Grill the chicken for 6-8 minutes on each side until fully cooked.
3. In the same pan, grill the bell peppers, zucchini, and cherry tomatoes for 5-7 minutes until tender.
4. Slice the grilled chicken and serve with the grilled vegetables.
5. Drizzle any remaining marinade over the top before serving.

Nutritional Information

Calories: 280, Protein: 35g, Carbohydrates: 12g, Fat: 10g, Fiber: 3g, Cholesterol: 85 mg, Salt: 300 mg, Potassium: 700 mg

HERB-ROASTED CHICKEN THIGHS

Servings 4 | Prep: 15 min | Cook: 35 min

These herb-roasted chicken thighs are juicy and flavorful, perfect for a heart-healthy meal. The blend of herbs and lemon adds a refreshing touch, making it a delightful dish for any occasion.

Equipment

Oven, Baking Tray, Mixing Bowl

Ingredients

- 800 g chicken thighs, skinless
- 30 ml olive oil
- 10 g fresh rosemary, chopped
- 10 g fresh thyme, chopped
- 2 cloves garlic, minced
- 1 lemon, sliced
- 5 g salt
- 3 g black pepper

Directions

1. Preheat the oven to 200°C (392°F).
2. In a mixing bowl, combine olive oil, rosemary, thyme, garlic, salt, and pepper.
3. Rub the herb mixture evenly over the chicken thighs.
4. Arrange the chicken thighs on a baking tray and place lemon slices on top.
5. Roast in the oven for 35 minutes or until the chicken is cooked through and golden brown.
6. Let rest for a few minutes before serving.

Nutritional Information

Calories: 320, Protein: 28g, Carbohydrates: 2g, Fat: 22g, Fiber: 1g, Cholesterol: 110 mg, Salt: 300 mg, Potassium: 350 mg

SPICY TANDOORI CHICKEN

Servings 4 | Prep: 15 min | Cook: 30 min

This Spicy Tandoori Chicken is a heart-healthy twist on the classic Indian dish, offering a flavorful and aromatic experience without the extra fat. Perfectly spiced and grilled to perfection, it's a delightful addition to any meal.

Equipment

Grill or Oven, Mixing Bowl, Measuring Spoons

Ingredients

- 600 g Chicken Breast, skinless
- 150 ml Low-Fat Yogurt
- 10 g Fresh Ginger, grated
- 10 g Garlic, minced
- 5 g Ground Cumin
- 5 g Ground Coriander
- 5 g Paprika
- 2 g Turmeric
- 2 g Cayenne Pepper
- 5 ml Lemon Juice
- 2 g Salt
- 5 g Fresh Cilantro, chopped (for garnish)

Directions

1. In a mixing bowl, combine yogurt, ginger, garlic, cumin, coriander, paprika, turmeric, cayenne pepper, lemon juice, and salt. Mix well to form a marinade.
2. Add the chicken breasts to the marinade, ensuring they are well coated. Cover and refrigerate for at least 1 hour, or overnight for best results.
3. Preheat the grill or oven to 200°C.
4. Grill the marinated chicken for 15 minutes on each side, or until fully cooked and slightly charred.
5. Garnish with fresh cilantro before serving.

Nutritional Information

Calories: 210, Protein: 35g, Carbohydrates: 6g, Fat: 4g, Fiber: 1g, Cholesterol: 85 mg, Salt: 500 mg, Potassium: 450 mg

CHICKEN AND QUINOA STIR-FRY

Servings 4 | Prep: 15 min | Cook: 20 min

This vibrant and nutritious stir-fry combines tender chicken with wholesome quinoa and colorful vegetables, making it a perfect heart-healthy meal.

Equipment

Wok or large skillet, Medium saucepan, Cutting board and knife

Ingredients

- 200 g chicken breast, thinly sliced
- 150 g quinoa
- 1 red bell pepper, sliced
- 100 g broccoli florets
- 50 g carrots, julienned
- 2 cloves garlic, minced
- 15 ml low-sodium soy sauce
- 10 ml olive oil
- 5 g fresh ginger, grated
- 250 ml water

Directions

1. Rinse quinoa under cold water. In a medium saucepan, combine quinoa and 250 ml water. Bring to a boil, then reduce heat to low, cover, and simmer for 15 minutes or until water is absorbed.
2. In a wok or large skillet, heat olive oil over medium heat. Add garlic and ginger, sauté for 1 minute until fragrant.
3. Add chicken slices to the wok, cooking until browned and cooked through, about 5-7 minutes.
4. Stir in bell pepper, broccoli, and carrots, cooking for another 5 minutes until vegetables are tender-crisp.
5. Add cooked quinoa and soy sauce to the wok, tossing everything together until well combined and heated through.

Nutritional Information

Calories: 320, Protein: 28g, Carbohydrates: 35g, Fat: 9g, Fiber: 6g, Cholesterol: 45 mg, Salt: 220 mg, Potassium: 620 mg

MEDITERRANEAN CHICKEN WRAP

Servings 4 | Prep: 15 min | Cook: 10 min

A delightful and heart-healthy wrap that combines tender chicken with fresh Mediterranean flavors, perfect for a quick lunch or light dinner.

Equipment

Grill pan, Mixing bowl, Knife

Ingredients

- 400 g boneless, skinless chicken breast
- 15 ml olive oil
- 5 g dried oregano
- 5 g garlic powder
- 2 g salt
- 4 whole wheat wraps (approximately 25 cm in diameter)
- 100 g cherry tomatoes, halved
- 50 g cucumber, sliced
- 50 g red onion, thinly sliced
- 50 g feta cheese, crumbled
- 30 g black olives, sliced
- 60 ml low-fat Greek yogurt
- 10 ml lemon juice

Directions

1. Preheat the grill pan over medium heat.
2. In a mixing bowl, coat the chicken breasts with olive oil, oregano, garlic powder, and salt.
3. Grill the chicken for about 5 minutes on each side, or until fully cooked. Remove and let rest for a few minutes before slicing thinly.
4. Lay out the whole wheat wraps and evenly distribute the sliced chicken, cherry tomatoes, cucumber, red onion, feta cheese, and black olives.
5. In a small bowl, mix the Greek yogurt with lemon juice and drizzle over the wraps.
6. Roll up each wrap tightly, slice in half, and serve immediately.

Nutritional Information

Calories: 350, Protein: 28g, Carbohydrates: 30g, Fat: 12g, Fiber: 6g, Cholesterol: 55 mg, Salt: 450 mg, Potassium: 500 mg

GRILLED CHICKEN WITH MANGO SALSA

Servings 4 | Prep: 15 min | Cook: 15 min

This vibrant and refreshing dish combines the lean protein of grilled chicken with the sweet and tangy flavors of mango salsa, making it a perfect heart-healthy meal.

Equipment

Grill pan, Mixing bowl, Tongs

Ingredients

- 500 g Chicken breast, boneless and skinless
- 15 ml Olive oil
- 5 g Ground cumin
- 2 g Salt
- 1 g Black pepper
- 200 g Mango, diced
- 50 g Red onion, finely chopped
- 50 g Red bell pepper, diced
- 15 ml Lime juice
- 10 g Fresh cilantro, chopped

Directions

1. Preheat the grill pan over medium-high heat.
2. Rub the chicken breasts with olive oil, cumin, salt, and black pepper.
3. Grill the chicken for 6-7 minutes on each side or until fully cooked.
4. In a mixing bowl, combine mango, red onion, red bell pepper, lime juice, and cilantro to make the salsa.
5. Serve the grilled chicken topped with mango salsa.

Nutritional Information

Calories: 280, Protein: 35g, Carbohydrates: 15g, Fat: 10g, Fiber: 3g, Cholesterol: 85 mg, Salt: 300 mg, Potassium: 600 mg

SPINACH AND FETA STUFFED CHICKEN

Servings 4 | Prep: 15 min | Cook: 30 min

This delightful dish combines tender chicken breasts with a savory spinach and feta filling, offering a heart-healthy meal that's both flavorful and satisfying.

Equipment

Oven, Skillet, Baking Dish

Ingredients

- 4 (150g each) Chicken Breasts
- 100g Fresh Spinach
- 100g Feta Cheese, crumbled
- 2 cloves Garlic, minced
- 15ml Olive Oil
- 5g Dried Oregano
- 2g Black Pepper
- 2g Salt

Directions

1. Preheat the oven to 180°C (350°F).
2. In a skillet, heat olive oil over medium heat. Add garlic and spinach, cooking until wilted.
3. Remove from heat and mix in feta cheese, oregano, salt, and pepper.
4. Cut a pocket into each chicken breast and stuff with the spinach mixture.
5. Place stuffed chicken in a baking dish and bake for 25-30 minutes, until cooked through.

Nutritional Information

Calories: 320, Protein: 40g, Carbohydrates: 3g, Fat: 17g, Fiber: 1g, Cholesterol: 100mg, Salt: 450mg, Potassium: 600mg

HONEY MUSTARD GLAZED CHICKEN

Servings 4 | Prep: 10 min | Cook: 25 min

This heart-healthy dish combines the sweetness of honey with the tang of mustard, creating a delightful glaze that enhances the natural flavors of the chicken. Perfect for a quick and nutritious meal.

Equipment

Oven, Baking dish, Mixing bowl

Ingredients

- 500 g chicken breast fillets
- 60 ml honey
- 60 ml Dijon mustard
- 15 ml olive oil
- 2 cloves garlic, minced
- 5 g fresh rosemary, chopped
- Salt and pepper to taste

Directions

1. Preheat the oven to 200°C.
2. In a mixing bowl, combine honey, Dijon mustard, olive oil, minced garlic, and chopped rosemary.
3. Season the chicken breasts with salt and pepper, then place them in a baking dish.
4. Pour the honey mustard mixture over the chicken, ensuring each piece is well coated.
5. Bake in the preheated oven for 25 minutes, or until the chicken is cooked through and the glaze is caramelized.
6. Let the chicken rest for a few minutes before serving.

Nutritional Information

Calories: 280, Protein: 30g, Carbohydrates: 18g, Fat: 10g, Fiber: 0g, Cholesterol: 75 mg, Salt: 180 mg, Potassium: 450 mg

GARLIC-LIME CHICKEN SKEWERS

Servings 4 | Prep: 15 min | Cook: 15 min

These Garlic-Lime Chicken Skewers are a zesty and flavorful option for a heart-healthy meal. The combination of garlic and lime infuses the chicken with a refreshing taste, perfect for grilling.

Equipment

Grill, Skewers, Mixing Bowl

Ingredients

- 500 g Chicken Breast, cut into cubes
- 3 cloves Garlic, minced
- 60 ml Fresh Lime Juice
- 15 ml Olive Oil
- 5 g Ground Cumin
- 2 g Salt
- 2 g Black Pepper
- 10 g Fresh Cilantro, chopped

Directions

1. In a mixing bowl, combine garlic, lime juice, olive oil, cumin, salt, and pepper.
2. Add chicken cubes to the marinade, ensuring they are well coated. Cover and refrigerate for at least 30 minutes.
3. Preheat the grill to medium-high heat.
4. Thread the marinated chicken onto skewers.
5. Grill the skewers for 12-15 minutes, turning occasionally, until the chicken is cooked through and slightly charred.
6. Garnish with fresh cilantro before serving.

Nutritional Information

Calories: 210, Protein: 30g, Carbohydrates: 3g, Fat: 8g, Fiber: 1g, Cholesterol: 75 mg, Salt: 500 mg, Potassium: 450 mg

SLOW COOKER CHICKEN AND VEGETABLES

Servings 4 | Prep: 15 min | Cook: 240 min

This heart-healthy slow cooker chicken and vegetables dish is a comforting and nutritious meal, perfect for busy days. The slow cooking process ensures tender chicken and flavorful vegetables, making it a family favorite.

Equipment

Slow Cooker, Cutting Board, Knife

Ingredients

- 500 g Chicken Breast, boneless and skinless
- 200 g Carrots, sliced
- 150 g Potatoes, diced
- 100 g Green Beans, trimmed
- 1 Onion, chopped
- 2 cloves Garlic, minced
- 200 ml Low-Sodium Chicken Broth
- 1 tbsp Olive Oil
- 1 tsp Dried Thyme
- 1 tsp Dried Rosemary
- Salt and Pepper to taste

Directions

1. Place the chicken breasts at the bottom of the slow cooker.
2. Add carrots, potatoes, green beans, onion, and garlic on top of the chicken.
3. Pour the chicken broth over the ingredients and drizzle with olive oil.
4. Sprinkle thyme, rosemary, salt, and pepper over the mixture.
5. Cover and cook on low for 4 hours or until the chicken is cooked through and vegetables are tender.

Nutritional Information

Calories: 320, Protein: 35g, Carbohydrates: 30g, Fat: 8g, Fiber: 5g, Cholesterol: 85 mg, Salt: 220 mg, Potassium: 950 mg

TURMERIC AND GINGER CHICKEN SOUP

Servings 4 | Prep: 15 min | Cook: 30 min

This vibrant and aromatic soup combines the anti-inflammatory properties of turmeric and ginger with lean chicken, creating a comforting and heart-healthy dish perfect for any season.

Equipment

Large Pot, Cutting Board, Knife

Ingredients

- 500 g chicken breast, diced
- 1 tablespoon olive oil
- 1 onion, finely chopped
- 2 cloves garlic, minced
- 20 g fresh ginger, grated
- 1 teaspoon ground turmeric
- 1 liter low-sodium chicken broth
- 200 g carrots, sliced
- 150 g celery, sliced
- 100 g spinach leaves
- Salt and pepper to taste
- 15 ml lemon juice

Directions

1. Heat olive oil in a large pot over medium heat. Add onion and garlic, sauté until translucent.
2. Stir in ginger and turmeric, cooking for 1 minute until fragrant.
3. Add chicken breast, cooking until lightly browned.
4. Pour in chicken broth, then add carrots and celery. Bring to a boil, reduce heat, and simmer for 20 minutes.
5. Stir in spinach and lemon juice, cooking for an additional 5 minutes. Season with salt and pepper.
6. Serve hot, garnished with fresh herbs if desired.

Nutritional Information

Calories: 250, Protein: 30g, Carbohydrates: 15g, Fat: 8g, Fiber: 4g, Cholesterol: 60 mg, Salt: 300 mg, Potassium: 700 mg

BAKED LEMON-HERB CHICKEN TENDERS

Servings 4 | Prep: 15 min | Cook: 20 min

These tender chicken strips are infused with zesty lemon and aromatic herbs, offering a delicious and heart-healthy option for any meal.

Equipment

Baking Sheet, Mixing Bowl, Oven

Ingredients

- 500 g Chicken Tenders
- 30 ml Olive Oil
- 1 Lemon, juiced and zested
- 5 g Dried Oregano
- 5 g Dried Thyme
- 2 g Garlic Powder
- 2 g Salt
- 1 g Black Pepper

Directions

1. Preheat the oven to 200°C (392°F) and line a baking sheet with parchment paper.
2. In a mixing bowl, combine olive oil, lemon juice, lemon zest, oregano, thyme, garlic powder, salt, and black pepper.
3. Add chicken tenders to the bowl and toss until well coated with the lemon-herb mixture.
4. Arrange the chicken tenders on the prepared baking sheet in a single layer.
5. Bake in the preheated oven for 18-20 minutes, or until the chicken is cooked through and golden brown.

Nutritional Information

Calories: 210, Protein: 28g, Carbohydrates: 2g, Fat: 10g, Fiber: 1g, Cholesterol: 70 mg, Salt: 300 mg, Potassium: 450 mg

GREEK CHICKEN WITH OLIVES

Servings 4 | Prep: 15 min | Cook: 30 min

This Greek-inspired dish combines tender chicken with the rich flavors of olives and herbs, offering a heart-healthy meal that's both satisfying and delicious.

Equipment

Skillet, Mixing Bowl, Tongs

Ingredients

- 500 g chicken breast, boneless and skinless
- 15 ml olive oil
- 100 g Kalamata olives, pitted and sliced
- 200 g cherry tomatoes, halved
- 1 lemon, juiced
- 5 g dried oregano
- 2 cloves garlic, minced
- 5 g fresh parsley, chopped
- Salt and pepper to taste

Directions

1. Heat olive oil in a skillet over medium heat.
2. Season chicken breasts with salt, pepper, and oregano.
3. Add chicken to the skillet and cook for 5-7 minutes on each side until golden brown and cooked through.
4. Remove chicken from skillet and set aside.
5. In the same skillet, add garlic, olives, and cherry tomatoes; sauté for 3-4 minutes.
6. Return chicken to the skillet, add lemon juice, and cook for an additional 2-3 minutes.
7. Garnish with fresh parsley before serving.

Nutritional Information

Calories: 320, Protein: 35g, Carbohydrates: 8g, Fat: 16g, Fiber: 3g, Cholesterol: 85 mg, Salt: 450 mg, Potassium: 750 mg

COCONUT LIME CHICKEN

Servings 4 | Prep: 15 min | Cook: 25 min

This Coconut Lime Chicken is a delightful blend of tropical flavors and tender poultry, perfect for a heart-healthy meal. The creamy coconut milk pairs beautifully with zesty lime, creating a dish that's both refreshing and satisfying.

Equipment

Skillet, Mixing Bowl, Measuring Cups and Spoons

Ingredients

- 500 g chicken breast, boneless and skinless
- 200 ml coconut milk, light
- 1 lime, juiced and zested
- 2 cloves garlic, minced
- 10 g fresh cilantro, chopped
- 5 g ground black pepper
- 5 g salt
- 15 ml olive oil

Directions

1. Slice the chicken breast into thin fillets.
2. In a mixing bowl, combine coconut milk, lime juice, lime zest, garlic, cilantro, black pepper, and salt.
3. Marinate the chicken in the mixture for at least 10 minutes.
4. Heat olive oil in a skillet over medium heat.
5. Cook the chicken fillets for 5-7 minutes on each side until golden brown and cooked through.
6. Pour the remaining marinade into the skillet and simmer for 5 minutes until slightly thickened.
7. Serve the chicken with the sauce drizzled on top, garnished with extra cilantro if desired.

Nutritional Information

Calories: 320, Protein: 28g, Carbohydrates: 5g, Fat: 20g, Fiber: 1g, Cholesterol: 70 mg, Salt: 300 mg, Potassium: 450 mg

CHICKEN AND CHICKPEA STEW

Servings 4 | Prep: 15 min | Cook: 30 min

This hearty and flavorful stew combines tender chicken with protein-rich chickpeas, making it a perfect heart-healthy meal.

Equipment

Large Pot, Wooden Spoon, Cutting Board

Ingredients

- 500 g Chicken Breast, diced
- 400 g Canned Chickpeas, drained and rinsed
- 200 g Tomatoes, chopped
- 1 Onion, diced
- 2 Garlic Cloves, minced
- 500 ml Low-Sodium Chicken Broth
- 10 ml Olive Oil
- 5 g Ground Cumin
- 5 g Paprika
- Salt and Pepper to taste
- Fresh Parsley, chopped (for garnish)

Directions

1. Heat olive oil in a large pot over medium heat. Add onion and garlic, sauté until soft.
2. Add diced chicken to the pot, cooking until browned on all sides.
3. Stir in tomatoes, chickpeas, cumin, and paprika. Cook for 2-3 minutes.
4. Pour in chicken broth, bring to a boil, then reduce heat and simmer for 20 minutes.
5. Season with salt and pepper to taste. Garnish with fresh parsley before serving.

Nutritional Information

Calories: 320, Protein: 35g, Carbohydrates: 28g, Fat: 8g, Fiber: 8g, Cholesterol: 65 mg, Salt: 300 mg, Potassium: 750 mg

HONEY GARLIC CHICKEN WITH BROCCOLI

Servings 4 | Prep: 10 min | Cook: 20 min

This delightful dish combines tender chicken with a sweet and savory honey garlic sauce, complemented by the freshness of broccoli. Perfect for a heart-healthy meal that doesn't compromise on flavor.

Equipment

Skillet, Mixing Bowl, Steamer or Pot with Steamer Basket

Ingredients

- 500 g chicken breast, cut into bite-sized pieces
- 200 g broccoli florets
- 60 ml honey
- 30 ml low-sodium soy sauce
- 15 ml olive oil
- 4 cloves garlic, minced
- 5 g cornstarch
- 30 ml water
- 2 g black pepper

Directions

1. In a mixing bowl, combine honey, soy sauce, minced garlic, and black pepper. Set aside.
2. Heat olive oil in a skillet over medium heat. Add chicken pieces and cook until golden brown, about 5-7 minutes.
3. Steam broccoli florets until tender, approximately 5 minutes.
4. Add the honey garlic mixture to the skillet with the chicken. Stir well to coat.
5. In a small bowl, mix cornstarch with water, then add to the skillet. Stir until the sauce thickens, about 2 minutes.
6. Add steamed broccoli to the skillet, toss to combine, and serve warm.

Nutritional Information

Calories: 320, Protein: 30g, Carbohydrates: 28g, Fat: 10g, Fiber: 3g, Cholesterol: 75 mg, Salt: 320 mg, Potassium: 600 mg

SMOKED PAPRIKA ROASTED CHICKEN

Servings 4 | Prep: 15 min | Cook: 45 min

This smoked paprika roasted chicken is a flavorful and heart-healthy dish, perfect for a comforting meal. The smoky aroma and tender meat make it a family favorite.

Equipment

Oven, Baking Tray, Mixing Bowl

Ingredients

- 1 kg Chicken, whole
- 15 g Smoked Paprika
- 10 g Garlic Powder
- 5 g Black Pepper
- 5 g Salt
- 30 ml Olive Oil
- 1 Lemon, sliced
- 10 g Fresh Thyme

Directions

1. Preheat the oven to 200°C (392°F).
2. In a mixing bowl, combine smoked paprika, garlic powder, black pepper, salt, and olive oil to form a paste.
3. Rub the paste evenly over the chicken, ensuring it is well-coated.
4. Place lemon slices and fresh thyme inside the chicken cavity.
5. Position the chicken on a baking tray and roast in the oven for 45 minutes, or until the internal temperature reaches 75°C (165°F).
6. Let the chicken rest for 10 minutes before carving and serving.

Nutritional Information

Calories: 320, Protein: 35g, Carbohydrates: 2g, Fat: 20g, Fiber: 1g, Cholesterol: 95 mg, Salt: 300 mg, Potassium: 450 mg

CHICKEN WITH ROASTED RED PEPPERS

Servings 4 | Prep: 15 min | Cook: 25 min

This dish combines tender chicken breast with the sweetness of roasted red peppers, creating a flavorful and heart-healthy meal.

Equipment

Skillet, Baking Sheet, Tongs

Ingredients

- 500 g chicken breast, boneless and skinless
- 200 g roasted red peppers, sliced
- 30 ml olive oil
- 2 cloves garlic, minced
- 5 g fresh basil, chopped
- 2 g black pepper
- 2 g salt

Directions

1. Preheat the oven to 200°C.
2. Season the chicken breasts with salt and black pepper.
3. Heat olive oil in a skillet over medium heat. Add garlic and sauté until fragrant.
4. Add chicken breasts to the skillet and cook for 5 minutes on each side until golden brown.
5. Transfer the chicken to a baking sheet and top with sliced roasted red peppers.
6. Bake in the preheated oven for 15 minutes, or until the chicken is cooked through.
7. Garnish with fresh basil before serving.

Nutritional Information

Calories: 250, Protein: 35g, Carbohydrates: 5g, Fat: 10g, Fiber: 2g, Cholesterol: 85 mg, Salt: 300 mg, Potassium: 600 mg

CRANBERRY WALNUT CHICKEN SALAD

Servings 4 | Prep: 15 min | Cook: 10 min

This delightful Cranberry Walnut Chicken Salad combines tender chicken with the sweetness of cranberries and the crunch of walnuts, making it a perfect heart-healthy meal.

Equipment

Mixing Bowl, Skillet, Measuring Cups and Spoons

Ingredients

- 400 g cooked chicken breast, shredded
- 60 g dried cranberries
- 50 g walnuts, chopped
- 100 g Greek yogurt
- 30 ml lemon juice
- 5 g Dijon mustard
- 50 g celery, diced
- 5 g fresh parsley, chopped
- Salt and pepper to taste

Directions

1. In a skillet, lightly toast the walnuts over medium heat for about 5 minutes, stirring frequently. Set aside to cool.
2. In a mixing bowl, combine Greek yogurt, lemon juice, and Dijon mustard. Mix until smooth.
3. Add shredded chicken, dried cranberries, toasted walnuts, diced celery, and chopped parsley to the bowl.
4. Gently fold the ingredients together until well combined.
5. Season with salt and pepper to taste.
6. Serve chilled or at room temperature.

Nutritional Information

Calories: 320, Protein: 28g, Carbohydrates: 18g, Fat: 15g, Fiber: 3g, Cholesterol: 70 mg, Salt: 180 mg, Potassium: 450 mg

LEMON-DIJON GRILLED CHICKEN

Servings 4 | Prep: 15 min | Cook: 20 min

This zesty Lemon-Dijon Grilled Chicken is a heart-healthy delight, combining the tang of lemon with the sharpness of Dijon mustard for a flavorful, juicy dish.

Equipment

Grill, Mixing Bowl, Whisk

Ingredients

- 500 g Chicken Breast Fillets
- 60 ml Fresh Lemon Juice
- 30 g Dijon Mustard
- 15 ml Olive Oil
- 2 cloves Garlic, minced
- 5 g Fresh Thyme Leaves
- 2 g Salt
- 1 g Black Pepper

Directions

1. In a mixing bowl, whisk together lemon juice, Dijon mustard, olive oil, minced garlic, fresh thyme, salt, and black pepper.
2. Place chicken breast fillets in the bowl, ensuring they are well-coated with the marinade. Cover and refrigerate for at least 30 minutes.
3. Preheat the grill to medium-high heat.
4. Remove chicken from marinade and place on the grill. Cook for 6-8 minutes on each side, or until the internal temperature reaches 75°C.
5. Let the chicken rest for a few minutes before serving to retain its juices.

Nutritional Information

Calories: 210, Protein: 35g, Carbohydrates: 2g, Fat: 7g, Fiber: 0g, Cholesterol: 85 mg, Salt: 250 mg, Potassium: 450 mg

CHICKEN AND ZUCCHINI SKILLET

Servings 4 | Prep: 10 min | Cook: 20 min

This delightful Chicken and Zucchini Skillet is a quick and nutritious meal, perfect for a heart-healthy diet. The combination of lean chicken and fresh zucchini creates a flavorful dish that's both satisfying and good for your heart.

Equipment

Skillet, Cutting Board, Knife

Ingredients

- 500 g Chicken breast, diced
- 300 g Zucchini, sliced
- 1 tbsp Olive oil (15 ml)
- 1 Onion, chopped (100 g)
- 2 Garlic cloves, minced
- 1 Red bell pepper, sliced (150 g)
- 1 tsp Dried oregano (5 g)
- Salt and pepper to taste
- 1 Lemon, juiced (50 ml)
- Fresh parsley, chopped (for garnish)

Directions

1. Heat olive oil in a skillet over medium heat. Add the onion and garlic, sauté until fragrant.
2. Add the diced chicken to the skillet, cooking until browned on all sides.
3. Stir in the zucchini and red bell pepper, cooking until vegetables are tender.
4. Season with oregano, salt, and pepper. Stir well to combine.
5. Drizzle lemon juice over the mixture, stirring to incorporate the flavors.
6. Remove from heat and garnish with fresh parsley before serving.

Nutritional Information

Calories: 250, Protein: 30g, Carbohydrates: 10g, Fat: 10g, Fiber: 3g, Cholesterol: 75 mg, Salt: 200 mg, Potassium: 600 mg

AVOCADO CHICKEN SALAD WRAP

Servings 4 | Prep: 15 min | Cook: 10 min

This Avocado Chicken Salad Wrap is a delightful blend of creamy avocado, tender chicken, and crisp vegetables, all wrapped up in a whole-grain tortilla. It's a heart-healthy meal that's both satisfying and nutritious.

Equipment

Mixing Bowl, Skillet, Knife

Ingredients

- 400 g cooked chicken breast, shredded
- 1 large avocado, peeled and diced
- 100 g Greek yogurt
- 50 g red onion, finely chopped
- 100 g cherry tomatoes, halved
- 1 tbsp lime juice
- 4 whole-grain tortillas
- 10 g fresh cilantro, chopped
- Salt and pepper to taste

Directions

1. In a mixing bowl, combine the shredded chicken, diced avocado, Greek yogurt, red onion, cherry tomatoes, and lime juice.
2. Season the mixture with salt and pepper to taste, then gently fold in the chopped cilantro.
3. Warm the whole-grain tortillas in a skillet over medium heat for about 1 minute on each side.
4. Divide the chicken salad mixture evenly among the tortillas.
5. Roll each tortilla tightly to form a wrap, securing with a toothpick if necessary.
6. Serve immediately or refrigerate for up to 2 hours before serving.

Nutritional Information

Calories: 320, Protein: 28g, Carbohydrates: 30g, Fat: 12g, Fiber: 8g, Cholesterol: 55 mg, Salt: 320 mg, Potassium: 680 mg

ORANGE GINGER GLAZED CHICKEN

Servings 4 | Prep: 15 min | Cook: 25 min

This dish combines the tangy sweetness of orange with the warm spice of ginger, creating a delightful glaze for tender chicken. Perfect for a heart-healthy meal that doesn't compromise on flavor.

Equipment

Skillet, Whisk, Measuring cups and spoons

Ingredients

- 500 g chicken breast, boneless and skinless
- 150 ml fresh orange juice
- 2 tablespoons (about 30 ml) low-sodium soy sauce
- 1 tablespoon (about 15 g) fresh ginger, grated
- 1 tablespoon (about 15 ml) honey
- 1 tablespoon (about 15 ml) olive oil
- 1 teaspoon (about 5 g) cornstarch
- 1 teaspoon (about 5 g) orange zest
- 1/2 teaspoon (about 2.5 g) black pepper

Directions

1. Slice the chicken breast into thin strips.
2. In a bowl, whisk together orange juice, soy sauce, ginger, honey, and cornstarch until smooth.
3. Heat olive oil in a skillet over medium heat. Add chicken strips and cook until golden brown, about 5 minutes.
4. Pour the orange-ginger mixture over the chicken. Stir well and cook until the sauce thickens and chicken is cooked through, about 10 minutes.
5. Sprinkle with orange zest and black pepper before serving.

Nutritional Information

Calories: 220, Protein: 30g, Carbohydrates: 15g, Fat: 5g, Fiber: 1g, Cholesterol: 75 mg, Salt: 300 mg, Potassium: 450 mg

SPICY PEANUT CHICKEN STIR-FRY

Servings 4 | Prep: 15 min | Cook: 20 min

This vibrant and flavorful stir-fry combines tender chicken with a spicy peanut sauce, offering a heart-healthy twist on a classic favorite.

Equipment

Wok or large skillet, Mixing bowl, Whisk

Ingredients

- 400 g chicken breast, thinly sliced
- 30 ml low-sodium soy sauce
- 15 ml sesame oil
- 100 g bell peppers, sliced
- 100 g broccoli florets
- 50 g carrots, julienned
- 60 ml natural peanut butter
- 10 ml sriracha sauce
- 5 g fresh ginger, grated
- 2 cloves garlic, minced
- 30 ml lime juice
- 15 g unsalted peanuts, chopped
- 15 g fresh cilantro, chopped

Directions

1. In a mixing bowl, whisk together peanut butter, soy sauce, sriracha, lime juice, ginger, and garlic to create the sauce.
2. Heat sesame oil in a wok over medium heat. Add chicken slices and stir-fry until cooked through, about 5-7 minutes.
3. Add bell peppers, broccoli, and carrots to the wok. Stir-fry for an additional 5 minutes until vegetables are tender-crisp.
4. Pour the peanut sauce over the chicken and vegetables. Stir well to coat everything evenly.
5. Garnish with chopped peanuts and cilantro before serving.

Nutritional Information

Calories: 320, Protein: 28g, Carbohydrates: 15g, Fat: 18g, Fiber: 4g, Cholesterol: 65 mg, Salt: 350 mg, Potassium: 650 mg

CUMIN AND CORIANDER CHICKEN

Servings 4 | Prep: 15 min | Cook: 25 min

This aromatic chicken dish combines the earthy flavors of cumin and coriander, creating a heart-healthy meal that's both delicious and satisfying.

Equipment

Skillet, Mixing Bowl, Measuring Spoons

Ingredients

- 500 g chicken breast, cut into strips
- 10 g ground cumin
- 10 g ground coriander
- 5 g garlic powder
- 5 g paprika
- 15 ml olive oil
- 1 lemon, juiced
- 5 g salt
- 2 g black pepper
- 100 ml low-sodium chicken broth
- 10 g fresh coriander, chopped

Directions

1. In a mixing bowl, combine cumin, coriander, garlic powder, paprika, salt, and pepper.
2. Add chicken strips to the bowl and coat evenly with the spice mixture.
3. Heat olive oil in a skillet over medium heat. Add chicken and cook until browned, about 5 minutes per side.
4. Pour in chicken broth and lemon juice, then cover and simmer for 15 minutes, until chicken is cooked through.
5. Garnish with fresh coriander before serving.

Nutritional Information

Calories: 220, Protein: 30g, Carbohydrates: 3g, Fat: 10g, Fiber: 1g, Cholesterol: 75 mg, Salt: 300 mg, Potassium: 450 mg

Seafood

GRILLED SALMON WITH LEMON AND DILL

Servings 4 | Prep: 10 min | Cook: 15 min

This heart-healthy grilled salmon is infused with the fresh flavors of lemon and dill, offering a delightful and nutritious meal perfect for any occasion.

Equipment

Grill, Mixing Bowl, Tongs

Ingredients

- 600 g Salmon Fillets
- 30 ml Olive Oil
- 1 Lemon, sliced
- 10 g Fresh Dill, chopped
- 5 g Garlic Powder
- 2 g Salt
- 2 g Black Pepper

Directions

1. Preheat the grill to medium-high heat.
2. In a mixing bowl, combine olive oil, garlic powder, salt, and black pepper.
3. Brush the salmon fillets with the olive oil mixture.
4. Place lemon slices and dill on top of each fillet.
5. Grill the salmon for 6-7 minutes on each side, or until cooked through.
6. Remove from grill and let rest for a few minutes before serving.

Nutritional Information

Calories: 320, Protein: 34g, Carbohydrates: 2g, Fat: 20g, Fiber: 1g, Cholesterol: 85 mg, Salt: 300 mg, Potassium: 750 mg

BAKED COD WITH GARLIC AND TOMATOES

Servings 4 | Prep: 10 min | Cook: 20 min

This dish combines tender cod fillets with the robust flavors of garlic and tomatoes, creating a heart-healthy meal that's both delicious and nutritious.

Equipment

Baking dish, Oven, Knife

Ingredients

- 600 g cod fillets
- 200 g cherry tomatoes, halved
- 30 ml olive oil
- 4 cloves garlic, minced
- 10 g fresh basil, chopped
- 5 g dried oregano
- 2 g salt
- 2 g black pepper

Directions

1. Preheat the oven to 200°C (392°F).
2. Place the cod fillets in a baking dish.
3. In a bowl, mix cherry tomatoes, olive oil, garlic, basil, oregano, salt, and pepper.
4. Pour the tomato mixture over the cod fillets, ensuring even coverage.
5. Bake in the preheated oven for 20 minutes, or until the cod is cooked through and flakes easily with a fork.

Nutritional Information

Calories: 250, Protein: 30g, Carbohydrates: 6g, Fat: 12g, Fiber: 2g, Cholesterol: 70 mg, Salt: 500 mg, Potassium: 800 mg

BLACKENED TILAPIA WITH LIME

Servings 4 | Prep: 10 min | Cook: 10 min

This zesty and flavorful blackened tilapia is a heart-healthy dish that combines the boldness of spices with the refreshing tang of lime, perfect for a quick and nutritious meal.

Equipment

Non-stick skillet, Mixing bowl, Spatula

Ingredients

- 600 g tilapia fillets
- 30 ml olive oil
- 10 g paprika
- 5 g garlic powder
- 5 g onion powder
- 5 g dried thyme
- 5 g dried oregano
- 2 g cayenne pepper
- 2 g black pepper
- 2 g salt
- 1 lime, cut into wedges

Directions

1. In a mixing bowl, combine paprika, garlic powder, onion powder, thyme, oregano, cayenne pepper, black pepper, and salt.
2. Brush tilapia fillets with olive oil on both sides.
3. Coat the fillets evenly with the spice mixture.
4. Heat a non-stick skillet over medium-high heat.
5. Cook the fillets for 3-4 minutes on each side until blackened and cooked through.
6. Serve immediately with lime wedges on the side.

Nutritional Information

Calories: 220, Protein: 35g, Carbohydrates: 2g, Fat: 9g, Fiber: 1g, Cholesterol: 75 mg, Salt: 500 mg, Potassium: 650 mg

GINGER SOY GLAZED SALMON

Servings 4 | Prep: 10 min | Cook: 15 min

This Ginger Soy Glazed Salmon is a delightful blend of savory and sweet flavors, offering a heart-healthy dish that's both delicious and nutritious.

Equipment

Baking Sheet, Mixing Bowl, Whisk

Ingredients

- 600 g Salmon Fillets
- 60 ml Low-Sodium Soy Sauce
- 30 ml Honey
- 15 g Fresh Ginger, grated
- 10 ml Olive Oil
- 2 Cloves Garlic, minced
- 5 g Sesame Seeds
- 2 Green Onions, sliced

Directions

1. Preheat the oven to 200°C and line a baking sheet with parchment paper.
2. In a mixing bowl, whisk together soy sauce, honey, ginger, olive oil, and garlic.
3. Place salmon fillets on the prepared baking sheet and brush generously with the ginger soy glaze.
4. Bake for 12-15 minutes, or until the salmon is cooked through and flakes easily with a fork.
5. Garnish with sesame seeds and sliced green onions before serving.

Nutritional Information

Calories: 320, Protein: 34g, Carbohydrates: 12g, Fat: 15g, Fiber: 1g, Cholesterol: 70 mg, Salt: 450 mg, Potassium: 750 mg

SHRIMP AND AVOCADO SALAD

Servings 4 | Prep: 15 min | Cook: 5 min

A refreshing and heart-healthy salad combining succulent shrimp with creamy avocado, perfect for a light lunch or dinner.

Equipment

Large skillet, Mixing bowl, Whisk

Ingredients

- 400 g shrimp, peeled and deveined
- 1 tbsp olive oil
- 1 avocado, diced
- 200 g cherry tomatoes, halved
- 50 g red onion, thinly sliced
- 30 ml lime juice
- 10 g fresh cilantro, chopped
- Salt and pepper to taste

Directions

1. Heat the olive oil in a large skillet over medium heat. Add the shrimp and cook for 2-3 minutes on each side until pink and opaque. Remove from heat and let cool.
2. In a mixing bowl, combine the lime juice, cilantro, salt, and pepper. Whisk to create the dressing.
3. Add the cooked shrimp, avocado, cherry tomatoes, and red onion to the bowl.
4. Gently toss all ingredients together until well coated with the dressing.
5. Serve immediately or chill for 10 minutes for enhanced flavors.

Nutritional Information

Calories: 250, Protein: 20g, Carbohydrates: 12g, Fat: 15g, Fiber: 5g, Cholesterol: 150 mg, Salt: 200 mg, Potassium: 600 mg

MISO-GLAZED HALIBUT

Servings 4 | Prep: 10 min | Cook: 15 min

This Miso-Glazed Halibut offers a perfect balance of savory and sweet flavors, making it a delightful heart-healthy dish. The tender halibut fillets are coated with a rich miso glaze, then broiled to perfection for a quick and nutritious meal.

Equipment

Baking Sheet, Mixing Bowl, Whisk

Ingredients

- 600 g Halibut Fillets
- 60 ml Miso Paste
- 30 ml Mirin
- 30 ml Rice Vinegar
- 15 ml Soy Sauce (low sodium)
- 10 g Fresh Ginger, grated
- 5 ml Sesame Oil
- 5 g Sesame Seeds
- 2 Green Onions, sliced

Directions

1. Preheat the oven to 200°C and line a baking sheet with parchment paper.
2. In a mixing bowl, whisk together the miso paste, mirin, rice vinegar, soy sauce, grated ginger, and sesame oil until smooth.
3. Place the halibut fillets on the prepared baking sheet and brush generously with the miso glaze.
4. Broil the fillets in the oven for 10-12 minutes, or until the fish is cooked through and the glaze is caramelized.
5. Garnish with sesame seeds and sliced green onions before serving.

Nutritional Information

Calories: 250, Protein: 30g, Carbohydrates: 10g, Fat: 8g, Fiber: 1g, Cholesterol: 60 mg, Salt: 400 mg, Potassium: 750 mg

GARLIC-LEMON SHRIMP SKEWERS

Servings 4 | Prep: 15 min | Cook: 10 min

These Garlic-Lemon Shrimp Skewers are a delightful heart-healthy option, bursting with zesty lemon and aromatic garlic flavors. Perfect for a quick and nutritious meal.

Equipment

Grill, Skewers, Mixing Bowl

Ingredients

- 500 g shrimp, peeled and deveined
- 3 cloves garlic, minced
- 60 ml lemon juice
- 30 ml olive oil
- 1 tsp lemon zest
- 1 tsp dried oregano
- Salt and pepper to taste
- Fresh parsley, chopped (for garnish)

Directions

1. In a mixing bowl, combine garlic, lemon juice, olive oil, lemon zest, oregano, salt, and pepper.
2. Add shrimp to the bowl and toss to coat evenly. Let marinate for 10 minutes.
3. Thread shrimp onto skewers.
4. Preheat grill to medium-high heat. Grill skewers for 2-3 minutes on each side, until shrimp are opaque and cooked through.
5. Garnish with fresh parsley before serving.

Nutritional Information

Calories: 210, Protein: 25g, Carbohydrates: 3g, Fat: 11g, Fiber: 0g, Cholesterol: 170 mg, Salt: 320 mg, Potassium: 220 mg

SEARED TUNA WITH SESAME CRUST

Servings 4 | Prep: 10 min | Cook: 6 min

This dish features perfectly seared tuna with a crunchy sesame crust, offering a delightful combination of textures and flavors. It's a quick and elegant meal that's heart-healthy and satisfying.

Equipment

Non-stick skillet, Mixing bowl, Tongs

Ingredients

- 500 g fresh tuna steaks
- 50 g white sesame seeds
- 50 g black sesame seeds
- 30 ml low-sodium soy sauce
- 15 ml olive oil
- 5 g freshly grated ginger
- 2 g black pepper

Directions

1. In a mixing bowl, combine white and black sesame seeds.
2. Coat the tuna steaks evenly with soy sauce, then press them into the sesame seed mixture to form a crust.
3. Heat olive oil in a non-stick skillet over medium-high heat.
4. Add the tuna steaks and sear for 2-3 minutes on each side, ensuring the center remains pink.
5. Remove from heat and let rest for a minute before slicing.
6. Serve with freshly grated ginger and a sprinkle of black pepper.

Nutritional Information

Calories: 280, Protein: 35g, Carbohydrates: 4g, Fat: 14g, Fiber: 2g, Cholesterol: 60 mg, Salt: 250 mg, Potassium: 600 mg

SCALLOPS WITH CITRUS DRESSING

Servings 4 | Prep: 15 min | Cook: 10 min

Delight in the fresh, zesty flavors of the sea with these perfectly seared scallops, complemented by a vibrant citrus dressing. This dish is not only heart-healthy but also a feast for the senses.

Equipment

Non-stick skillet, Mixing bowl, Whisk

Ingredients

- 400 g scallops
- 30 ml olive oil
- 1 orange, juiced
- 1 lemon, juiced
- 1 lime, juiced
- 10 g fresh parsley, chopped
- 2 cloves garlic, minced
- 2 g black pepper
- 2 g salt

Directions

1. Pat the scallops dry with a paper towel and season with salt and black pepper.
2. Heat olive oil in a non-stick skillet over medium-high heat.
3. Add scallops to the skillet and sear for 2-3 minutes on each side until golden brown and opaque in the center. Remove from heat.
4. In a mixing bowl, combine orange juice, lemon juice, lime juice, minced garlic, and chopped parsley. Whisk together to make the citrus dressing.
5. Drizzle the citrus dressing over the seared scallops and serve immediately.

Nutritional Information

Calories: 210, Protein: 22g, Carbohydrates: 6g, Fat: 10g, Fiber: 1g, Cholesterol: 40 mg, Salt: 300 mg, Potassium: 450 mg

HERB-CRUSTED BAKED FISH

Servings 4 | Prep: 15 min | Cook: 20 min

This dish features tender fish fillets coated with a flavorful herb crust, offering a delicious and heart-healthy meal that's both simple and satisfying.

Equipment

Baking Sheet, Mixing Bowl, Oven

Ingredients

- 600 g white fish fillets (such as cod or haddock)
- 50 g whole wheat breadcrumbs
- 30 g fresh parsley, chopped
- 10 g fresh dill, chopped
- 2 cloves garlic, minced
- 30 ml olive oil
- 1 lemon, zested and juiced
- Salt and pepper to taste

Directions

1. Preheat the oven to 200°C (392°F) and line a baking sheet with parchment paper.
2. In a mixing bowl, combine breadcrumbs, parsley, dill, garlic, lemon zest, and olive oil. Season with salt and pepper.
3. Pat the fish fillets dry with a paper towel and place them on the prepared baking sheet.
4. Spread the herb mixture evenly over the top of each fillet, pressing gently to adhere.
5. Bake in the preheated oven for 15-20 minutes, or until the fish is cooked through and the crust is golden brown.
6. Drizzle with lemon juice before serving.

Nutritional Information

Calories: 250, Protein: 30g, Carbohydrates: 10g, Fat: 10g, Fiber: 2g, Cholesterol: 60 mg, Salt: 150 mg, Potassium: 600 mg

MEDITERRANEAN SHRIMP STIR-FRY

Servings 4 | Prep: 15 min | Cook: 10 min

This vibrant Mediterranean Shrimp Stir-Fry combines succulent shrimp with fresh vegetables and aromatic herbs, delivering a heart-healthy meal that's both delicious and nutritious.

Equipment

Large Skillet, Mixing Bowl, Spatula

Ingredients

- 400 g shrimp, peeled and deveined
- 200 g cherry tomatoes, halved
- 150 g bell peppers, sliced
- 100 g zucchini, sliced
- 50 g red onion, thinly sliced
- 30 ml olive oil
- 2 cloves garlic, minced
- 5 g dried oregano
- 5 g dried basil
- 30 ml lemon juice
- Salt and pepper to taste

Directions

1. Heat olive oil in a large skillet over medium heat.
2. Add garlic and red onion, sauté until fragrant.
3. Stir in shrimp, cooking until they turn pink.
4. Add cherry tomatoes, bell peppers, and zucchini; cook until vegetables are tender.
5. Sprinkle oregano, basil, salt, and pepper; stir well.
6. Drizzle with lemon juice before serving.

Nutritional Information

Calories: 220, Protein: 25g, Carbohydrates: 10g, Fat: 10g, Fiber: 3g, Cholesterol: 150 mg, Salt: 300 mg, Potassium: 450 mg

TERIYAKI SALMON WITH BROWN RICE

Servings 4 | Prep: 15 min | Cook: 20 min

This dish combines the rich flavors of teriyaki-glazed salmon with the nutty taste of brown rice, creating a heart-healthy meal that's both delicious and satisfying.

Equipment

Oven, Saucepan, Baking Sheet

Ingredients

- 600 g Salmon fillets
- 200 ml Teriyaki sauce
- 250 g Brown rice
- 500 ml Water
- 1 tbsp Olive oil
- 100 g Broccoli florets
- 1 tsp Sesame seeds

Directions

1. Preheat the oven to 200°C (392°F).
2. In a saucepan, bring 500 ml of water to a boil, add the brown rice, reduce heat, and simmer for 20 minutes until tender.
3. Place salmon fillets on a baking sheet, brush with olive oil, and pour teriyaki sauce over them.
4. Bake the salmon in the preheated oven for 15-20 minutes until cooked through.
5. Steam broccoli florets until tender, about 5 minutes.
6. Serve the salmon over a bed of brown rice, garnished with steamed broccoli and sesame seeds.

Nutritional Information

Calories: 450, Protein: 35g, Carbohydrates: 45g, Fat: 15g, Fiber: 5g, Cholesterol: 70 mg, Salt: 800 mg, Potassium: 750 mg

POACHED COD IN TOMATO BROTH

Servings 4 | Prep: 10 min | Cook: 20 min

This dish features tender cod fillets gently poached in a rich, aromatic tomato broth, offering a heart-healthy and flavorful meal that's both satisfying and nutritious.

Equipment

Large saucepan, Cutting board, Knife

Ingredients

- 600 g cod fillets
- 15 ml olive oil
- 1 onion, finely chopped
- 2 garlic cloves, minced
- 400 g canned diced tomatoes
- 500 ml low-sodium vegetable broth
- 5 g dried oregano
- 5 g dried basil
- Salt and pepper to taste
- 10 g fresh parsley, chopped (for garnish)

Directions

1. Heat olive oil in a large saucepan over medium heat. Add the onion and garlic, sauté until softened.
2. Stir in the canned tomatoes, vegetable broth, oregano, and basil. Season with salt and pepper. Bring to a simmer.
3. Gently place the cod fillets into the tomato broth. Cover and poach for 10-12 minutes, or until the fish is cooked through and flakes easily with a fork.
4. Taste and adjust seasoning if necessary.
5. Serve the poached cod in bowls with the tomato broth, garnished with fresh parsley.

Nutritional Information

Calories: 220, Protein: 30g, Carbohydrates: 12g, Fat: 5g, Fiber: 3g, Cholesterol: 60 mg, Salt: 150 mg, Potassium: 850 mg

GRILLED MAHI-MAHI WITH PINEAPPLE SALSA

Servings 4 | Prep: 15 min | Cook: 10 min

This vibrant dish combines the rich flavor of grilled mahi-mahi with a refreshing pineapple salsa, perfect for a heart-healthy meal that delights the senses.

Equipment

Grill, Mixing Bowl, Tongs

Ingredients

- 600 g mahi-mahi fillets
- 15 ml olive oil
- 2 g salt
- 1 g black pepper
- 200 g fresh pineapple, diced
- 50 g red onion, finely chopped
- 30 g red bell pepper, diced
- 15 ml lime juice
- 10 g fresh cilantro, chopped

Directions

1. Preheat the grill to medium-high heat.
2. Brush the mahi-mahi fillets with olive oil and season with salt and black pepper.
3. Grill the fillets for 4-5 minutes on each side until cooked through and slightly charred.
4. In a mixing bowl, combine pineapple, red onion, red bell pepper, lime juice, and cilantro to make the salsa.
5. Serve the grilled mahi-mahi topped with pineapple salsa.

Nutritional Information

Calories: 220, Protein: 30g, Carbohydrates: 12g, Fat: 7g, Fiber: 2g, Cholesterol: 80 mg, Salt: 300 mg, Potassium: 750 mg

DIJON MUSTARD ROASTED TROUT

Servings 4 | Prep: 10 min | Cook: 15 min

This dish features tender trout fillets coated with a tangy Dijon mustard glaze, roasted to perfection. It's a simple yet flavorful way to enjoy heart-healthy seafood.

Equipment

Baking Sheet, Mixing Bowl, Brush

Ingredients

- 600 g Trout Fillets
- 60 ml Dijon Mustard
- 30 ml Olive Oil
- 10 g Fresh Dill, chopped
- 5 g Garlic Powder
- 5 g Lemon Zest
- 2 g Salt
- 1 g Black Pepper

Directions

1. Preheat your oven to 200°C (392°F).
2. In a mixing bowl, combine Dijon mustard, olive oil, fresh dill, garlic powder, lemon zest, salt, and black pepper.
3. Place the trout fillets on a baking sheet lined with parchment paper.
4. Brush the mustard mixture evenly over the trout fillets.
5. Roast in the preheated oven for 12-15 minutes, or until the trout is cooked through and flakes easily with a fork.
6. Serve immediately, garnished with additional dill if desired.

Nutritional Information

Calories: 280, Protein: 30g, Carbohydrates: 2g, Fat: 18g, Fiber: 0g, Cholesterol: 70 mg, Salt: 300 mg, Potassium: 550 mg

SPICY GARLIC SHRIMP

Servings 4 | Prep: 10 min | Cook: 10 min

This Spicy Garlic Shrimp recipe is a delightful blend of heat and flavor, perfect for a heart-healthy meal that doesn't compromise on taste. Quick to prepare, it's an ideal choice for a nutritious weeknight dinner.

Equipment

Skillet, Mixing Bowl, Spatula

Ingredients

- 500 g Shrimp, peeled and deveined
- 30 ml Olive Oil
- 4 cloves Garlic, minced
- 5 g Red Pepper Flakes
- 15 ml Lemon Juice
- 5 g Fresh Parsley, chopped
- Salt and Pepper to taste

Directions

1. Heat olive oil in a skillet over medium heat.
2. Add minced garlic and red pepper flakes, sauté for 1 minute until fragrant.
3. Add shrimp to the skillet, cooking for 2-3 minutes on each side until pink and opaque.
4. Drizzle with lemon juice and season with salt and pepper.
5. Garnish with fresh parsley before serving.

Nutritional Information

Calories: 210, Protein: 25g, Carbohydrates: 2g, Fat: 12g, Fiber: 0g, Cholesterol: 170 mg, Salt: 300 mg, Potassium: 220 mg

ALMOND-CRUSTED TILAPIA

Servings 4 | Prep: 15 min | Cook: 15 min

This almond-crusted tilapia offers a delightful crunch and a nutty flavor, making it a perfect heart-healthy dish that's both delicious and nutritious.

Equipment

Baking Sheet, Mixing Bowl, Food Processor

Ingredients

- 4 fillets (about 600 g) Tilapia
- 100 g Almonds
- 50 g Whole Wheat Bread Crumbs
- 2 g Garlic Powder
- 2 g Paprika
- 2 g Salt
- 1 g Black Pepper
- 30 ml Olive Oil
- 1 Lemon, sliced

Directions

1. Preheat the oven to 200°C and line a baking sheet with parchment paper.
2. In a food processor, pulse almonds until finely ground. Transfer to a mixing bowl and combine with bread crumbs, garlic powder, paprika, salt, and black pepper.
3. Brush each tilapia fillet with olive oil, then press into the almond mixture, ensuring an even coating.
4. Place the coated fillets on the prepared baking sheet and bake for 12-15 minutes, or until the fish flakes easily with a fork.
5. Serve immediately with lemon slices on the side.

Nutritional Information

Calories: 320, Protein: 35g, Carbohydrates: 10g, Fat: 18g, Fiber: 3g, Cholesterol: 60 mg, Salt: 300 mg, Potassium: 500 mg

SMOKED SALMON AND CUCUMBER ROLLS

Servings 4 | Prep: 15 min | Cook: 0 min

These refreshing smoked salmon and cucumber rolls are perfect for a light appetizer or snack. The combination of creamy cheese, fresh cucumber, and savory smoked salmon offers a delightful taste and texture, while being heart-healthy.

Equipment

Cutting Board, Knife, Vegetable Peeler

Ingredients

- 200 g Smoked Salmon
- 1 Cucumber
- 100 g Low-Fat Cream Cheese
- 10 g Fresh Dill, chopped
- 5 ml Lemon Juice
- 1 g Black Pepper

Directions

1. Slice the cucumber lengthwise into thin strips using a vegetable peeler.
2. In a bowl, mix the cream cheese, chopped dill, lemon juice, and black pepper until smooth.
3. Spread a thin layer of the cream cheese mixture onto each cucumber strip.
4. Place a slice of smoked salmon on top of the cream cheese layer.
5. Roll the cucumber strip tightly and secure with a toothpick if necessary.
6. Repeat with the remaining cucumber strips and salmon.
7. Serve immediately or chill for a few minutes before serving.

Nutritional Information

Calories: 120, Protein: 10g, Carbohydrates: 4g, Fat: 7g, Fiber: 1g, Cholesterol: 25mg, Salt: 300mg, Potassium: 250mg

TUNA AND WHITE BEAN SALAD

Servings 4 | Prep: 15 min | Cook: 0 min

This refreshing Tuna and White Bean Salad is a perfect blend of protein-rich tuna and fiber-packed beans, tossed with fresh vegetables and a zesty dressing, making it a heart-healthy choice for any meal.

Equipment

Mixing Bowl, Strainer, Whisk

Ingredients

- 200 g canned tuna, drained
- 400 g canned white beans, rinsed and drained
- 150 g cherry tomatoes, halved
- 50 g red onion, finely chopped
- 30 g fresh parsley, chopped
- 50 ml extra virgin olive oil
- 30 ml lemon juice
- 5 g Dijon mustard
- Salt and pepper to taste

Directions

1. In a mixing bowl, combine the drained tuna and white beans.
2. Add the cherry tomatoes, red onion, and parsley to the bowl.
3. In a separate small bowl, whisk together the olive oil, lemon juice, Dijon mustard, salt, and pepper.
4. Pour the dressing over the tuna and bean mixture.
5. Gently toss all ingredients until well combined.
6. Serve immediately or refrigerate for up to 2 hours to allow flavors to meld.

Nutritional Information

Calories: 320, Protein: 25g, Carbohydrates: 28g, Fat: 14g, Fiber: 8g, Cholesterol: 25 mg, Salt: 300 mg, Potassium: 600 mg

LEMON HERB BAKED SCALLOPS

Servings 4 | Prep: 10 min | Cook: 15 min

Delight in the fresh and zesty flavors of lemon and herbs paired with tender scallops, a perfect heart-healthy dish that's both simple and elegant.

Equipment

Baking Dish, Mixing Bowl, Oven

Ingredients

- 500 g scallops
- 30 ml olive oil
- 2 cloves garlic, minced
- 1 lemon, juiced and zested
- 10 g fresh parsley, chopped
- 5 g fresh thyme, chopped
- 2 g salt
- 1 g black pepper

Directions

1. Preheat the oven to 200°C (392°F).
2. In a mixing bowl, combine olive oil, garlic, lemon juice, lemon zest, parsley, thyme, salt, and pepper.
3. Add scallops to the bowl and gently toss to coat them evenly with the herb mixture.
4. Arrange the scallops in a single layer in a baking dish.
5. Bake in the preheated oven for 12-15 minutes, until scallops are opaque and cooked through.
6. Garnish with additional parsley before serving, if desired.

Nutritional Information

Calories: 180, Protein: 20g, Carbohydrates: 4g, Fat: 9g, Fiber: 1g, Cholesterol: 40 mg, Salt: 200 mg, Potassium: 450 mg

STEAMED MUSSELS IN WHITE WINE

Servings 4 | Prep: 10 min | Cook: 10 min

A delightful and heart-healthy dish, these steamed mussels are infused with the aromatic flavors of white wine, garlic, and herbs, offering a light yet satisfying meal.

Equipment

Large Pot, Lid, Strainer

Ingredients

- 1 kg fresh mussels, cleaned and debearded
- 250 ml dry white wine
- 2 cloves garlic, minced
- 1 medium onion, finely chopped
- 15 g fresh parsley, chopped
- 30 ml olive oil
- 1 lemon, cut into wedges
- Salt and pepper to taste

Directions

1. Heat olive oil in a large pot over medium heat. Add the onion and garlic, sautéing until the onion is translucent.
2. Pour in the white wine and bring to a simmer.
3. Add the mussels to the pot, cover with a lid, and steam for 5-7 minutes, or until the mussels have opened.
4. Discard any mussels that do not open. Stir in the fresh parsley and season with salt and pepper.
5. Serve immediately with lemon wedges on the side.

Nutritional Information

Calories: 250, Protein: 24g, Carbohydrates: 10g, Fat: 10g, Fiber: 1g, Cholesterol: 60 mg, Salt: 300 mg, Potassium: 450 mg

SARDINE AND TOMATO BRUSCHETTA

Servings 4 | Prep: 10 min | Cook: 5 min

This vibrant and heart-healthy bruschetta combines the rich flavors of sardines with the freshness of tomatoes, creating a delightful appetizer that's both nutritious and satisfying.

Equipment

Grill pan, Mixing bowl, Spoon

Ingredients

- 200 g canned sardines in olive oil, drained
- 150 g cherry tomatoes, diced
- 1 clove garlic, minced
- 30 ml extra virgin olive oil
- 10 g fresh basil leaves, chopped
- 4 slices whole-grain bread
- 5 ml balsamic vinegar
- Salt and pepper to taste

Directions

1. Preheat the grill pan over medium heat.
2. In a mixing bowl, combine the sardines, cherry tomatoes, garlic, olive oil, basil, and balsamic vinegar. Season with salt and pepper.
3. Grill the bread slices for about 2 minutes on each side until they are golden and crispy.
4. Top each slice of bread with the sardine and tomato mixture.
5. Serve immediately, garnished with additional basil if desired.

Nutritional Information

Calories: 250, Protein: 12g, Carbohydrates: 22g, Fat: 14g, Fiber: 4g, Cholesterol: 30 mg, Salt: 220 mg, Potassium: 350 mg

OVEN-ROASTED HALIBUT WITH ROSEMARY

Servings 4 | Prep: 10 min | Cook: 20 min

This dish features tender halibut fillets infused with the earthy aroma of rosemary, creating a simple yet elegant heart-healthy meal.

Equipment

Baking Sheet, Parchment Paper, Oven

Ingredients

- 600 g Halibut Fillets
- 2 tbsp Olive Oil (approximately 30 ml)
- 1 tbsp Fresh Rosemary, chopped (approximately 5 g)
- 1 Lemon, sliced
- 1 tsp Sea Salt (approximately 5 g)
- 1/2 tsp Black Pepper (approximately 2 g)

Directions

1. Preheat the oven to 200°C (392°F). Line a baking sheet with parchment paper.
2. Place the halibut fillets on the prepared baking sheet.
3. Drizzle olive oil over the fillets and sprinkle with chopped rosemary, sea salt, and black pepper.
4. Arrange lemon slices on top of the fillets.
5. Roast in the preheated oven for 15-20 minutes, or until the fish flakes easily with a fork.

Nutritional Information

Calories: 250, Protein: 35g, Carbohydrates: 2g, Fat: 12g, Fiber: 0g, Cholesterol: 60 mg, Salt: 300 mg, Potassium: 750 mg

BAKED TROUT WITH ALMONDS

Servings 4 | Prep: 10 min | Cook: 25 min

This dish features tender trout fillets baked to perfection and topped with crunchy almonds, offering a delightful blend of flavors and textures that are both heart-healthy and satisfying.

Equipment

Baking Sheet, Mixing Bowl, Oven

Ingredients

- 4 (150g each) Trout Fillets
- 30g Sliced Almonds
- 15ml Olive Oil
- 1 Lemon, sliced
- 5g Fresh Parsley, chopped
- 2g Salt
- 1g Black Pepper

Directions

1. Preheat the oven to 180°C (356°F).
2. Place the trout fillets on a baking sheet lined with parchment paper.
3. Drizzle olive oil over the fillets and season with salt and black pepper.
4. Sprinkle sliced almonds evenly over the top of each fillet.
5. Arrange lemon slices around the fillets for added flavor.
6. Bake in the preheated oven for 20-25 minutes, or until the trout is cooked through and flakes easily with a fork.
7. Garnish with fresh parsley before serving.

Nutritional Information

Calories: 320, Protein: 35g, Carbohydrates: 3g, Fat: 20g, Fiber: 1g, Cholesterol: 80mg, Salt: 250mg, Potassium: 650mg

CILANTRO LIME SHRIMP BOWL

Servings 4 | Prep: 15 min | Cook: 10 min

This vibrant and zesty shrimp bowl is a heart-healthy delight, combining the freshness of cilantro and lime with succulent shrimp. Perfect for a quick, nutritious meal.

Equipment

Skillet, Mixing Bowl, Cutting Board

Ingredients

- 500 g shrimp, peeled and deveined
- 30 ml olive oil
- 3 cloves garlic, minced
- 1 lime, juiced and zested
- 10 g fresh cilantro, chopped
- 200 g brown rice, cooked
- 100 g cherry tomatoes, halved
- 1 avocado, sliced
- Salt and pepper to taste

Directions

1. In a mixing bowl, combine shrimp, olive oil, garlic, lime juice, lime zest, salt, and pepper. Toss to coat evenly.
2. Heat a skillet over medium heat. Add the shrimp mixture and cook for 3-4 minutes on each side until shrimp are pink and opaque.
3. Divide cooked brown rice among four bowls.
4. Top each bowl with cooked shrimp, cherry tomatoes, avocado slices, and chopped cilantro.
5. Serve immediately, garnished with additional lime wedges if desired.

Nutritional Information

Calories: 350, Protein: 25g, Carbohydrates: 30g, Fat: 15g, Fiber: 6g, Cholesterol: 150 mg, Salt: 300 mg, Potassium: 700 mg

MEDITERRANEAN GRILLED OCTOPUS

Servings 4 | Prep: 20 min | Cook: 40 min

This Mediterranean Grilled Octopus is a heart-healthy delight, offering a perfect blend of tender octopus with zesty lemon and aromatic herbs, capturing the essence of coastal cuisine.

Equipment

Large Pot, Grill or Grill Pan, Tongs

Ingredients

- 1 kg Fresh Octopus
- 60 ml Olive Oil
- 2 Lemons (juiced)
- 4 Garlic Cloves (minced)
- 5 g Fresh Oregano (chopped)
- 5 g Fresh Parsley (chopped)
- 2 g Sea Salt
- 2 g Black Pepper

Directions

1. Clean the octopus thoroughly under cold water.
2. In a large pot, bring water to a boil and simmer the octopus for 30 minutes until tender.
3. Remove the octopus, let it cool slightly, and cut into manageable pieces.
4. In a bowl, mix olive oil, lemon juice, garlic, oregano, parsley, salt, and pepper.
5. Marinate the octopus pieces in the mixture for 10 minutes.
6. Preheat the grill to medium-high heat.
7. Grill the octopus for 3-5 minutes on each side until charred and fragrant.

Nutritional Information

Calories: 250, Protein: 30g, Carbohydrates: 5g, Fat: 12g, Fiber: 1g, Cholesterol: 95 mg, Salt: 500 mg, Potassium: 450 mg

Vegetarian Meals

LENTIL AND SWEET POTATO CURRY

Servings 4 | Prep: 15 min | Cook: 30 min

This hearty and flavorful curry combines the earthiness of lentils with the sweetness of sweet potatoes, creating a comforting and nutritious meal perfect for heart health.

Equipment

Large Pot, Wooden Spoon, Knife

Ingredients

- 200 g red lentils
- 400 g sweet potatoes, peeled and diced
- 1 onion, finely chopped
- 2 cloves garlic, minced
- 15 ml olive oil
- 400 ml low-sodium vegetable broth
- 200 ml coconut milk
- 10 g curry powder
- 5 g ground cumin
- 5 g ground coriander
- 5 g turmeric
- Salt and pepper to taste
- Fresh cilantro for garnish

Directions

1. Heat olive oil in a large pot over medium heat. Add the onion and garlic, sauté until the onion is translucent.
2. Stir in the curry powder, cumin, coriander, and turmeric, cooking for 1 minute until fragrant.
3. Add the sweet potatoes and lentils, stirring to coat them with the spices.
4. Pour in the vegetable broth and bring to a boil. Reduce heat, cover, and simmer for 20 minutes.
5. Stir in the coconut milk, season with salt and pepper, and simmer for an additional 10 minutes until the sweet potatoes are tender.
6. Serve hot, garnished with fresh cilantro.

Nutritional Information

Calories: 350, Protein: 12g, Carbohydrates: 55g, Fat: 10g, Fiber: 12g, Cholesterol: 0 mg, Salt: 150 mg, Potassium: 800 mg

QUINOA AND BLACK BEAN TACOS

Servings 4 | Prep: 15 min | Cook: 20 min

These Quinoa and Black Bean Tacos are a delicious and heart-healthy twist on a classic favorite. Packed with protein and fiber, they offer a satisfying and nutritious meal perfect for any day of the week.

Equipment

Medium Saucepan, Large Skillet, Mixing Bowl

Ingredients

- 150 g Quinoa
- 400 ml Water
- 1 tbsp Olive Oil
- 1 small Onion, chopped
- 2 cloves Garlic, minced
- 1 tsp Ground Cumin
- 1 tsp Paprika
- 400 g Black Beans, drained and rinsed
- 200 g Cherry Tomatoes, halved
- 1 Lime, juiced
- 8 Corn Tortillas
- 50 g Fresh Cilantro, chopped

Directions

1. Rinse quinoa under cold water. In a medium saucepan, combine quinoa and water. Bring to a boil, reduce heat, and simmer for 15 minutes until water is absorbed.
2. In a large skillet, heat olive oil over medium heat. Add onion and garlic, sauté until softened.
3. Stir in cumin and paprika, cooking for an additional minute.
4. Add black beans and cherry tomatoes to the skillet, cooking until heated through. Stir in cooked quinoa and lime juice.
5. Warm tortillas in a dry skillet or microwave. Fill each tortilla with the quinoa mixture and top with fresh cilantro.

Nutritional Information

Calories: 320, Protein: 12g, Carbohydrates: 55g, Fat: 8g, Fiber: 12g, Cholesterol: 0 mg, Salt: 10 mg, Potassium: 650 mg

CHICKPEA AND SPINACH STIR-FRY

Servings 4 | Prep: 10 min | Cook: 15 min

This vibrant and flavorful stir-fry combines the earthy taste of chickpeas with the freshness of spinach, creating a heart-healthy meal that's both satisfying and nutritious.

Equipment

Large Skillet, Wooden Spoon, Measuring Cups and Spoons

Ingredients

- 400 g canned chickpeas, drained and rinsed
- 200 g fresh spinach leaves
- 1 medium onion, thinly sliced
- 2 cloves garlic, minced
- 15 ml olive oil
- 5 g ground cumin
- 5 g ground coriander
- 2 g salt
- 2 g black pepper
- 15 ml lemon juice

Directions

1. Heat the olive oil in a large skillet over medium heat.
2. Add the sliced onion and garlic, sautéing until the onion becomes translucent.
3. Stir in the cumin and coriander, cooking for an additional minute until fragrant.
4. Add the chickpeas to the skillet, stirring to coat them with the spices.
5. Toss in the spinach leaves, cooking until they wilt, about 3-4 minutes.
6. Season with salt, pepper, and lemon juice, stirring well to combine.
7. Serve warm, garnished with additional lemon wedges if desired.

Nutritional Information

Calories: 210, Protein: 9g, Carbohydrates: 30g, Fat: 7g, Fiber: 8g, Cholesterol: 0 mg, Salt: 300 mg, Potassium: 600 mg

STUFFED BELL PEPPERS WITH BROWN RICE

Servings 4 | Prep: 15 min | Cook: 40 min

These vibrant stuffed bell peppers are filled with a hearty mixture of brown rice, vegetables, and spices, making for a satisfying and heart-healthy meal.

Equipment

Oven, Baking dish, Medium saucepan, Mixing bowl

Ingredients

- 4 large bell peppers
- 200 g cooked brown rice
- 150 g canned black beans, drained and rinsed
- 100 g corn kernels
- 1 small onion, chopped
- 2 cloves garlic, minced
- 1 tsp olive oil
- 1 tsp ground cumin
- 1 tsp smoked paprika
- 100 g diced tomatoes
- Salt and pepper to taste

Directions

1. Preheat the oven to 180°C (350°F).
2. Cut the tops off the bell peppers and remove the seeds. Place them in a baking dish.
3. In a medium saucepan, heat olive oil over medium heat. Sauté onion and garlic until soft.
4. Add cooked brown rice, black beans, corn, diced tomatoes, cumin, smoked paprika, salt, and pepper. Stir to combine and heat through.
5. Stuff each bell pepper with the rice mixture.
6. Cover the baking dish with foil and bake for 30 minutes. Remove foil and bake for an additional 10 minutes.

Nutritional Information

Calories: 250, Protein: 8g, Carbohydrates: 45g, Fat: 4g, Fiber: 10g, Cholesterol: 0 mg, Salt: 300 mg, Potassium: 600 mg

BAKED EGGPLANT PARMESAN

Servings 4 | Prep: 20 min | Cook: 30 min

This heart-healthy version of the classic Italian dish is baked instead of fried, offering a deliciously crispy and cheesy experience without the extra oil.

Equipment

Baking Sheet, Oven, Mixing Bowl

Ingredients

- 500 g Eggplant, sliced into 1 cm rounds
- 200 g Tomato Sauce
- 100 g Mozzarella Cheese, shredded
- 50 g Parmesan Cheese, grated
- 100 g Whole Wheat Bread Crumbs
- 2 g Dried Oregano
- 2 g Dried Basil
- 5 ml Olive Oil
- Salt and Pepper to taste

Directions

1. Preheat the oven to 200°C (392°F).
2. Arrange eggplant slices on a baking sheet and brush lightly with olive oil. Season with salt and pepper.
3. Bake for 15 minutes, flipping halfway through, until tender and slightly golden.
4. In a mixing bowl, combine bread crumbs, oregano, and basil.
5. Spread a thin layer of tomato sauce on each eggplant slice, sprinkle with the bread crumb mixture, and top with mozzarella and Parmesan cheese.
6. Return to the oven and bake for an additional 15 minutes, until the cheese is melted and bubbly.
7. Serve warm, garnished with fresh basil if desired.

Nutritional Information

Calories: 250, Protein: 12g, Carbohydrates: 30g, Fat: 10g, Fiber: 8g, Cholesterol: 20 mg, Salt: 300 mg, Potassium: 600 mg

SPAGHETTI SQUASH WITH TOMATO BASIL SAUCE

Servings 4 | Prep: 15 min | Cook: 45 min

This delightful dish combines the unique texture of spaghetti squash with a fresh and flavorful tomato basil sauce, making it a perfect heart-healthy meal.

Equipment

Oven, Baking Sheet, Saucepan

Ingredients

- 1 kg spaghetti squash
- 15 ml olive oil
- 400 g canned diced tomatoes
- 2 cloves garlic, minced
- 10 g fresh basil leaves, chopped
- 5 g dried oregano
- Salt and pepper to taste

Directions

1. Preheat the oven to 200°C. Cut the spaghetti squash in half lengthwise and remove the seeds.
2. Drizzle the cut sides with olive oil and place face down on a baking sheet. Roast for 35-40 minutes until tender.
3. In a saucepan, heat a little olive oil over medium heat. Add minced garlic and sauté until fragrant.
4. Stir in the canned tomatoes, oregano, salt, and pepper. Simmer for 10 minutes.
5. Remove the squash from the oven and use a fork to scrape out the strands.
6. Mix the spaghetti squash strands with the tomato sauce and top with fresh basil before serving.

Nutritional Information

Calories: 180, Protein: 4g, Carbohydrates: 30g, Fat: 6g, Fiber: 7g, Cholesterol: 0 mg, Salt: 120 mg, Potassium: 650 mg

CAULIFLOWER AND CHICKPEA MASALA

Servings 4 | Prep: 15 min | Cook: 30 min

This vibrant and aromatic Cauliflower and Chickpea Masala is a heart-healthy dish that combines tender cauliflower florets and protein-rich chickpeas in a fragrant tomato-based sauce. Perfect for a comforting meal that's both nutritious and satisfying.

Equipment

Large Pot, Wooden Spoon, Knife

Ingredients

- 500 g Cauliflower, cut into florets
- 400 g Canned Chickpeas, drained and rinsed
- 200 g Tomatoes, chopped
- 150 g Onion, finely chopped
- 2 cloves Garlic, minced
- 15 g Fresh Ginger, grated
- 15 ml Olive Oil
- 10 g Garam Masala
- 5 g Ground Cumin
- 5 g Ground Coriander
- 5 g Turmeric Powder
- 5 g Salt
- 250 ml Vegetable Broth
- 15 g Fresh Cilantro, chopped (for garnish)

Directions

1. Heat olive oil in a large pot over medium heat. Add the onion, garlic, and ginger, sautéing until the onion is translucent.
2. Stir in the garam masala, cumin, coriander, turmeric, and salt, cooking for 1 minute until fragrant.
3. Add the chopped tomatoes and cook for 5 minutes, allowing them to soften.
4. Mix in the cauliflower florets and chickpeas, ensuring they are well coated with the spice mixture.
5. Pour in the vegetable broth, bring to a simmer, and cover. Cook for 20 minutes, or until the cauliflower is tender.
6. Garnish with fresh cilantro before serving.

Nutritional Information

Calories: 220, Protein: 10g, Carbohydrates: 35g, Fat: 7g, Fiber: 10g, Cholesterol: 0 mg, Salt: 600 mg, Potassium: 700 mg

MEDITERRANEAN LENTIL AND FETA WRAP

Servings 4 | Prep: 15 min | Cook: 25 min

This Mediterranean Lentil and Feta Wrap is a delightful blend of flavors and textures, offering a heart-healthy meal that's both satisfying and nutritious.

Equipment

Saucepan, Mixing Bowl, Spoon

Ingredients

- 200 g cooked lentils
- 100 g feta cheese, crumbled
- 1 medium cucumber, diced
- 150 g cherry tomatoes, halved
- 50 g red onion, finely chopped
- 60 ml olive oil
- 30 ml lemon juice
- 4 whole wheat wraps
- 10 g fresh parsley, chopped
- Salt and pepper to taste

Directions

1. In a saucepan, cook lentils according to package instructions, then drain and let cool.
2. In a mixing bowl, combine cooked lentils, feta cheese, cucumber, cherry tomatoes, and red onion.
3. In a small bowl, whisk together olive oil, lemon juice, salt, and pepper. Pour over the lentil mixture and toss to combine.
4. Lay out the whole wheat wraps and evenly distribute the lentil mixture onto each wrap.
5. Sprinkle fresh parsley over the top, then roll each wrap tightly.
6. Serve immediately or refrigerate for up to 2 hours before serving.

Nutritional Information

Calories: 320, Protein: 12g, Carbohydrates: 40g, Fat: 14g, Fiber: 8g, Cholesterol: 15 mg, Salt: 420 mg, Potassium: 450 mg

SWEET POTATO AND BLACK BEAN ENCHILADAS

Servings 4 | Prep: 20 min | Cook: 30 min

These enchiladas are a delightful fusion of sweet and savory, packed with nutrients and flavor, perfect for a heart-healthy meal.

Equipment

Oven, Baking Dish, Skillet

Ingredients

- 500 g sweet potatoes, peeled and diced
- 1 tbsp olive oil
- 1 onion, chopped
- 2 cloves garlic, minced
- 400 g canned black beans, drained and rinsed
- 200 ml tomato sauce
- 8 corn tortillas
- 100 g low-fat cheese, grated
- 1 tsp cumin
- 1 tsp chili powder
- Salt and pepper to taste
- Fresh cilantro for garnish

Directions

1. Preheat the oven to 180°C.
2. In a skillet, heat olive oil over medium heat. Add onions and garlic, sauté until translucent.
3. Add sweet potatoes, cumin, chili powder, salt, and pepper. Cook until sweet potatoes are tender.
4. Stir in black beans and 100 ml of tomato sauce, cook for 5 minutes.
5. Fill each tortilla with the sweet potato mixture, roll, and place seam-side down in a baking dish.
6. Pour remaining tomato sauce over the enchiladas and sprinkle with cheese.
7. Bake for 20 minutes or until cheese is bubbly. Garnish with cilantro before serving.

Nutritional Information

Calories: 350, Protein: 12g, Carbohydrates: 55g, Fat: 9g, Fiber: 12g, Cholesterol: 10 mg, Salt: 300 mg, Potassium: 800 mg

ROASTED VEGETABLE AND HUMMUS WRAP

Servings 4 | Prep: 15 min | Cook: 25 min

This vibrant wrap combines the rich flavors of roasted vegetables with creamy hummus, offering a satisfying and heart-healthy meal perfect for any time of the day.

Equipment

Oven, Baking Sheet, Knife, Cutting Board

Ingredients

- 200 g mixed bell peppers, sliced
- 150 g zucchini, sliced
- 150 g eggplant, sliced
- 2 tbsp olive oil
- 1 tsp dried oregano
- 200 g hummus
- 4 whole grain wraps
- 50 g fresh spinach leaves
- Salt and pepper to taste

Directions

1. Preheat the oven to 200°C (392°F).
2. On a baking sheet, toss the bell peppers, zucchini, and eggplant with olive oil, oregano, salt, and pepper.
3. Roast the vegetables in the oven for 20-25 minutes until tender and slightly caramelized.
4. Spread 50 g of hummus evenly over each wrap.
5. Layer the roasted vegetables and fresh spinach leaves on top of the hummus.
6. Roll the wraps tightly, slice in half, and serve immediately.

Nutritional Information

Calories: 320, Protein: 8g, Carbohydrates: 40g, Fat: 15g, Fiber: 8g, Cholesterol: 0 mg, Salt: 300 mg, Potassium: 600 mg

ZUCCHINI NOODLES WITH AVOCADO PESTO

Servings 4 | Prep: 15 min | Cook: 5 min

A refreshing and creamy dish, Zucchini Noodles with Avocado Pesto offers a delightful twist on traditional pasta, perfect for a heart-healthy meal.

Equipment

Spiralizer, Blender, Large Skillet

Ingredients

- 800 g Zucchini
- 2 ripe Avocados
- 30 g Fresh Basil Leaves
- 30 g Pine Nuts
- 2 cloves Garlic
- 60 ml Olive Oil
- 15 ml Lemon Juice
- Salt and Pepper to taste

Directions

1. Use a spiralizer to turn the zucchini into noodles and set aside.
2. In a blender, combine avocados, basil leaves, pine nuts, garlic, olive oil, lemon juice, salt, and pepper. Blend until smooth.
3. Heat a large skillet over medium heat. Add the zucchini noodles and sauté for 2-3 minutes until slightly tender.
4. Remove the skillet from heat and toss the zucchini noodles with the avocado pesto until well coated.
5. Serve immediately, garnished with additional pine nuts or basil if desired.

Nutritional Information

Calories: 320, Protein: 5g, Carbohydrates: 14g, Fat: 29g, Fiber: 9g, Cholesterol: 0 mg, Salt: 150 mg, Potassium: 900 mg

HEARTY THREE-BEAN CHILI

Servings 4 | Prep: 15 min | Cook: 30 min

This robust and flavorful chili combines three types of beans with a medley of spices, offering a heart-healthy and satisfying meal perfect for any occasion.

Equipment

Large Pot, Wooden Spoon, Measuring Cups and Spoons

Ingredients

- 15 ml Olive Oil
- 1 Onion, chopped (about 150 g)
- 2 Garlic Cloves, minced
- 1 Red Bell Pepper, chopped (about 150 g)
- 400 g Canned Diced Tomatoes
- 250 g Canned Kidney Beans, drained and rinsed
- 250 g Canned Black Beans, drained and rinsed
- 250 g Canned Pinto Beans, drained and rinsed
- 500 ml Vegetable Broth
- 15 g Chili Powder
- 5 g Ground Cumin
- 5 g Smoked Paprika
- Salt and Pepper to taste

Directions

1. Heat olive oil in a large pot over medium heat. Add onion and garlic, sauté until onion is translucent.
2. Stir in red bell pepper and cook for another 3 minutes.
3. Add diced tomatoes, kidney beans, black beans, and pinto beans to the pot.
4. Pour in vegetable broth and add chili powder, cumin, and smoked paprika. Stir well.
5. Bring the mixture to a boil, then reduce heat and let it simmer for 20 minutes, stirring occasionally.
6. Season with salt and pepper to taste before serving.

Nutritional Information

Calories: 320, Protein: 15g, Carbohydrates: 55g, Fat: 5g, Fiber: 15g, Cholesterol: 0 mg, Salt: 480 mg, Potassium: 900 mg

MUSHROOM AND SPINACH QUICHE

Servings 4 | Prep: 20 min | Cook: 35 min

This heart-healthy quiche combines the earthy flavors of mushrooms with the vibrant taste of spinach, all encased in a light, whole-grain crust. Perfect for a nutritious breakfast or a satisfying lunch.

Equipment

Oven, Skillet, Mixing Bowl, Quiche Pan

Ingredients

- 200 g Mushrooms, sliced
- 150 g Fresh Spinach
- 1 tbsp Olive Oil
- 3 Large Eggs
- 100 ml Low-Fat Milk
- 100 g Whole-Grain Flour
- 50 g Low-Fat Cheese, grated
- 1 tsp Baking Powder
- Salt and Pepper to taste

Directions

1. Preheat the oven to 180°C (350°F).
2. In a skillet, heat olive oil over medium heat. Sauté mushrooms until golden, then add spinach and cook until wilted.
3. In a mixing bowl, whisk together eggs, milk, flour, baking powder, salt, and pepper. Stir in the cheese.
4. Add the sautéed mushrooms and spinach to the egg mixture, stirring until well combined.
5. Pour the mixture into a greased quiche pan and bake for 30-35 minutes, or until the center is set and the top is golden.

Nutritional Information

Calories: 220, Protein: 12g, Carbohydrates: 18g, Fat: 10g, Fiber: 3g, Cholesterol: 140 mg, Salt: 220 mg, Potassium: 450 mg

BROCCOLI AND TOFU STIR-FRY

Servings 4 | Prep: 10 min | Cook: 15 min

This vibrant and nutritious stir-fry combines the crunch of broccoli with the protein-rich goodness of tofu, all tossed in a savory sauce. It's a quick and satisfying meal perfect for any night of the week.

Equipment

Wok or large frying pan, Knife, Cutting board

Ingredients

- 300 g firm tofu, cubed
- 300 g broccoli florets
- 1 tablespoon (15 ml) olive oil
- 2 cloves garlic, minced
- 1 tablespoon (15 ml) low-sodium soy sauce
- 1 tablespoon (15 ml) sesame oil
- 1 teaspoon (5 g) grated ginger
- 1 red bell pepper, sliced
- 50 ml water

Directions

1. Heat the olive oil in a wok over medium heat. Add the tofu cubes and stir-fry until golden brown, about 5 minutes. Remove and set aside.
2. In the same wok, add garlic and ginger, stir-frying for 1 minute until fragrant.
3. Add broccoli florets and red bell pepper to the wok, stir-frying for 3-4 minutes.
4. Return the tofu to the wok, add soy sauce, sesame oil, and water. Stir well to combine.
5. Cook for another 3-4 minutes until the broccoli is tender-crisp. Serve hot.

Nutritional Information

Calories: 180, Protein: 12g, Carbohydrates: 14g, Fat: 10g, Fiber: 5g, Cholesterol: 0 mg, Salt: 200 mg, Potassium: 450 mg

ROASTED BUTTERNUT SQUASH AND KALE BOWL

Servings 4 | Prep: 15 min | Cook: 30 min

This vibrant and nourishing bowl combines the sweetness of roasted butternut squash with the earthy flavors of kale, creating a heart-healthy meal that's both satisfying and delicious.

Equipment

Baking Sheet, Large Mixing Bowl, Oven

Ingredients

- 800 g Butternut Squash, peeled and cubed
- 200 g Kale, chopped
- 30 ml Olive Oil
- 5 g Garlic Powder
- 5 g Paprika
- 2 g Salt
- 2 g Black Pepper
- 50 g Quinoa, cooked
- 30 ml Lemon Juice

Directions

1. Preheat the oven to 200°C (392°F).
2. In a large mixing bowl, toss the butternut squash cubes with olive oil, garlic powder, paprika, salt, and black pepper.
3. Spread the seasoned squash evenly on a baking sheet and roast for 25 minutes, or until tender and slightly caramelized.
4. Meanwhile, massage the chopped kale with lemon juice and a pinch of salt in the mixing bowl until it softens.
5. Once the squash is roasted, combine it with the kale and cooked quinoa in the mixing bowl.
6. Toss everything together gently to combine and serve warm.

Nutritional Information

Calories: 220, Protein: 5g, Carbohydrates: 35g, Fat: 8g, Fiber: 7g, Cholesterol: 0 mg, Salt: 300 mg, Potassium: 800 mg

CHICKPEA AND QUINOA STUFFED TOMATOES

Servings 4 | Prep: 15 min | Cook: 30 min

These vibrant stuffed tomatoes are a delightful blend of protein-rich chickpeas and quinoa, offering a heart-healthy meal that's both satisfying and delicious.

Equipment

Baking Tray, Medium Saucepan, Mixing Bowl

Ingredients

- 4 large tomatoes
- 150 g cooked quinoa
- 200 g canned chickpeas, drained and rinsed
- 50 g red onion, finely chopped
- 30 g fresh parsley, chopped
- 1 clove garlic, minced
- 15 ml olive oil
- 5 g ground cumin
- Salt and pepper to taste

Directions

1. Preheat the oven to 180°C (350°F).
2. Slice the tops off the tomatoes and scoop out the insides, setting them aside.
3. In a mixing bowl, combine quinoa, chickpeas, onion, parsley, garlic, olive oil, cumin, and the reserved tomato insides. Season with salt and pepper.
4. Stuff each tomato with the quinoa mixture and place them on a baking tray.
5. Bake for 25-30 minutes, until the tomatoes are tender and the filling is heated through.

Nutritional Information

Calories: 210, Protein: 8g, Carbohydrates: 32g, Fat: 6g, Fiber: 8g, Cholesterol: 0 mg, Salt: 150 mg, Potassium: 600 mg

BAKED FALAFEL WITH TAHINI DRESSING

Servings 4 | Prep: 20 min | Cook: 25 min

Savor the delightful crunch of baked falafel paired with a creamy tahini dressing, perfect for a heart-healthy meal that doesn't compromise on flavor.

Equipment

Baking Sheet, Food Processor, Mixing Bowl

Ingredients

- 400 g Canned Chickpeas, drained and rinsed
- 50 g Red Onion, roughly chopped
- 2 cloves Garlic
- 15 g Fresh Parsley
- 15 g Fresh Cilantro
- 5 g Ground Cumin
- 5 g Ground Coriander
- 5 g Baking Powder
- 30 g Whole Wheat Flour
- 30 ml Olive Oil
- 60 ml Tahini
- 30 ml Lemon Juice
- 1 clove Garlic, minced
- 60 ml Water
- Salt and Pepper to taste

Directions

1. Preheat the oven to 200°C and line a baking sheet with parchment paper.
2. In a food processor, combine chickpeas, onion, garlic, parsley, cilantro, cumin, coriander, baking powder, and flour. Pulse until a coarse mixture forms.
3. Shape the mixture into small balls and place them on the prepared baking sheet. Brush with olive oil.
4. Bake for 20-25 minutes, turning halfway through, until golden and crisp.
5. For the dressing, whisk together tahini, lemon juice, minced garlic, and water in a mixing bowl. Season with salt and pepper.
6. Serve the baked falafel warm, drizzled with tahini dressing.

Nutritional Information

Calories: 320, Protein: 12g, Carbohydrates: 40g, Fat: 14g, Fiber: 10g, Cholesterol: 0 mg, Salt: 150 mg, Potassium: 450 mg

GREEK-STYLE STUFFED PEPPERS

Servings 4 | Prep: 15 min | Cook: 30 min

These Greek-style stuffed peppers are a delightful blend of Mediterranean flavors, offering a heart-healthy and satisfying vegetarian meal.

Equipment

Oven, Baking Dish, Mixing Bowl

Ingredients

- 4 large bell peppers (about 800g total)
- 200g cooked quinoa
- 150g feta cheese, crumbled
- 100g cherry tomatoes, halved
- 50g black olives, sliced
- 30g red onion, finely chopped
- 15ml olive oil
- 5g dried oregano
- Salt and pepper to taste

Directions

1. Preheat the oven to 180°C. Cut the tops off the bell peppers and remove the seeds.
2. In a mixing bowl, combine quinoa, feta cheese, cherry tomatoes, olives, red onion, olive oil, oregano, salt, and pepper.
3. Stuff each bell pepper with the quinoa mixture, pressing down gently to fill completely.
4. Place the stuffed peppers in a baking dish and cover with foil.
5. Bake in the preheated oven for 25-30 minutes, until the peppers are tender.
6. Remove the foil for the last 5 minutes of baking to lightly brown the tops.
7. Serve warm, garnished with fresh herbs if desired.

Nutritional Information

Calories: 280, Protein: 10g, Carbohydrates: 30g, Fat: 14g, Fiber: 6g, Cholesterol: 25mg, Salt: 400mg, Potassium: 600mg

SPICED LENTIL AND CARROT PATTIES

Servings 4 | Prep: 15 min | Cook: 20 min

These spiced lentil and carrot patties are a delicious and heart-healthy option, packed with flavor and nutrients. Perfect for a light lunch or dinner, they offer a satisfying texture and a hint of spice.

Equipment

Mixing Bowl, Frying Pan, Food Processor

Ingredients

- 200 g red lentils
- 150 g carrots, grated
- 1 onion, finely chopped
- 2 cloves garlic, minced
- 50 g whole wheat breadcrumbs
- 10 g ground cumin
- 10 g ground coriander
- 5 g smoked paprika
- 15 ml olive oil
- Salt and pepper to taste

Directions

1. Cook the lentils in boiling water for about 10 minutes until tender, then drain and set aside.
2. In a food processor, combine the cooked lentils, grated carrots, onion, garlic, breadcrumbs, cumin, coriander, paprika, salt, and pepper. Pulse until the mixture is well combined but still slightly chunky.
3. Shape the mixture into 8 patties.
4. Heat olive oil in a frying pan over medium heat. Cook the patties for 4-5 minutes on each side until golden brown and heated through.
5. Serve warm with a side salad or whole grain buns.

Nutritional Information

Calories: 230, Protein: 10g, Carbohydrates: 35g, Fat: 6g, Fiber: 10g, Cholesterol: 0 mg, Salt: 150 mg, Potassium: 500 mg

PORTOBELLO MUSHROOM AND AVOCADO BURGER

Servings 4 | Prep: 15 min | Cook: 10 min

A hearty and flavorful burger that combines the meaty texture of portobello mushrooms with creamy avocado, perfect for a heart-healthy meal.

Equipment

Grill pan, Mixing bowl, Spatula

Ingredients

- 4 large portobello mushrooms (approximately 400g total)
- 2 tablespoons (30ml) olive oil
- 1 teaspoon (5g) garlic powder
- 1 teaspoon (5g) smoked paprika
- 2 avocados (approximately 300g total), peeled and sliced
- 4 whole-grain burger buns (approximately 240g total)
- 1 tomato (approximately 150g), sliced
- 50g baby spinach leaves
- Salt and pepper to taste

Directions

1. Preheat the grill pan over medium heat.
2. Brush the portobello mushrooms with olive oil and season with garlic powder, smoked paprika, salt, and pepper.
3. Grill the mushrooms for 4-5 minutes on each side until tender.
4. Toast the burger buns on the grill for 1-2 minutes until lightly browned.
5. Assemble the burgers by layering spinach, grilled mushrooms, avocado slices, and tomato on the buns.

Nutritional Information

Calories: 320, Protein: 8g, Carbohydrates: 38g, Fat: 18g, Fiber: 10g, Cholesterol: 0mg, Salt: 220mg, Potassium: 900mg

VEGAN SHEPHERD'S PIE WITH MASHED CAULIFLOWER

Servings 4 | Prep: 20 min | Cook: 40 min

This comforting Vegan Shepherd's Pie swaps traditional mashed potatoes for creamy mashed cauliflower, making it a heart-healthy and deliciously satisfying meal.

Equipment

Oven, Large Pot, Baking Dish, Blender or Food Processor

Ingredients

- 1 kg cauliflower, chopped
- 200 ml unsweetened almond milk
- 2 tbsp olive oil
- 1 onion, diced
- 2 cloves garlic, minced
- 300 g carrots, diced
- 200 g peas
- 400 g canned lentils, drained and rinsed
- 250 ml vegetable broth
- 1 tbsp tomato paste
- 1 tsp dried thyme
- Salt and pepper to taste

Directions

1. Preheat the oven to 200°C.
2. Boil the cauliflower in a large pot of salted water until tender, about 10 minutes. Drain and blend with almond milk until smooth.
3. In a large pan, heat olive oil over medium heat. Sauté onion and garlic until fragrant.
4. Add carrots, peas, lentils, vegetable broth, tomato paste, and thyme. Simmer for 10 minutes.
5. Transfer the vegetable mixture to a baking dish. Spread the mashed cauliflower evenly on top.
6. Bake for 20 minutes or until the top is golden.
7. Let cool slightly before serving.

Nutritional Information

Calories: 280, Protein: 12g, Carbohydrates: 45g, Fat: 8g, Fiber: 14g, Cholesterol: 0 mg, Salt: 300 mg, Potassium: 950 mg

MOROCCAN CHICKPEA AND COUSCOUS BOWL

Servings 4 | Prep: 15 min | Cook: 20 min

This vibrant Moroccan-inspired bowl combines the earthy flavors of chickpeas and the light, fluffy texture of couscous, enhanced with aromatic spices and fresh herbs for a heart-healthy meal.

Equipment

Medium Saucepan, Large Mixing Bowl, Skillet

Ingredients

- 200 g Couscous
- 400 g Canned Chickpeas, drained and rinsed
- 1 Medium Red Bell Pepper, diced
- 1 Medium Zucchini, diced
- 1 Medium Red Onion, finely chopped
- 2 Cloves Garlic, minced
- 15 ml Olive Oil
- 5 g Ground Cumin
- 5 g Ground Coriander
- 2 g Ground Cinnamon
- 500 ml Vegetable Broth
- 30 g Fresh Parsley, chopped
- Salt and Pepper to taste

Directions

1. In a medium saucepan, bring the vegetable broth to a boil. Remove from heat, add couscous, cover, and let it sit for 5 minutes. Fluff with a fork.
2. In a skillet, heat olive oil over medium heat. Add red onion and garlic, sauté until fragrant.
3. Add red bell pepper and zucchini to the skillet, cook until softened.
4. Stir in chickpeas, cumin, coriander, and cinnamon. Cook for another 5 minutes, stirring occasionally.
5. Combine the cooked couscous with the chickpea mixture in a large mixing bowl. Season with salt and pepper.
6. Garnish with fresh parsley before serving.

Nutritional Information

Calories: 320, Protein: 10g, Carbohydrates: 55g, Fat: 8g, Fiber: 10g, Cholesterol: 0 mg, Salt: 480 mg, Potassium: 600 mg

BLACK BEAN AND CORN-STUFFED SWEET POTATOES

Servings 4 | Prep: 15 min | Cook: 45 min

These Black Bean and Corn-Stuffed Sweet Potatoes are a delightful blend of flavors and textures, offering a hearty and nutritious meal that's perfect for heart health.

Equipment

Oven, Baking Sheet, Mixing Bowl

Ingredients

- 4 medium sweet potatoes (about 800g total)
- 200g canned black beans, drained and rinsed
- 150g corn kernels (fresh or frozen)
- 1 small red onion, finely chopped (about 70g)
- 1 red bell pepper, diced (about 120g)
- 1 tsp ground cumin
- 1 tsp smoked paprika
- 30ml olive oil
- Salt and pepper to taste
- Fresh cilantro for garnish (optional)

Directions

1. Preheat the oven to 200°C. Pierce each sweet potato several times with a fork and place them on a baking sheet.
2. Bake the sweet potatoes for 40-45 minutes, or until tender.
3. In a mixing bowl, combine black beans, corn, red onion, red bell pepper, cumin, smoked paprika, olive oil, salt, and pepper. Mix well.
4. Once the sweet potatoes are cooked, let them cool slightly, then slice them open lengthwise.
5. Stuff each sweet potato with the black bean and corn mixture.
6. Return the stuffed sweet potatoes to the oven for an additional 5 minutes to heat through.
7. Garnish with fresh cilantro before serving, if desired.

Nutritional Information

Calories: 320, Protein: 8g, Carbohydrates: 60g, Fat: 8g, Fiber: 12g, Cholesterol: 0mg, Salt: 150mg, Potassium: 950mg

ROASTED BRUSSELS SPROUTS WITH QUINOA AND CRANBERRIES

Servings 4 | Prep: 10 min | Cook: 25 min

This vibrant dish combines the earthy flavors of roasted Brussels sprouts with the nutty texture of quinoa and the sweet-tart burst of cranberries, creating a heart-healthy and satisfying meal.

Equipment

Oven, Baking Sheet, Saucepan

Ingredients

- 500 g Brussels sprouts, halved
- 15 ml olive oil
- 1 g salt
- 1 g black pepper
- 200 g quinoa
- 500 ml water
- 50 g dried cranberries
- 30 g chopped walnuts
- 15 ml lemon juice

Directions

1. Preheat the oven to 200°C.
2. Toss Brussels sprouts with olive oil, salt, and pepper. Spread on a baking sheet and roast for 20 minutes, until golden and tender.
3. Meanwhile, rinse quinoa under cold water. In a saucepan, combine quinoa and water. Bring to a boil, then reduce heat and simmer for 15 minutes, or until water is absorbed.
4. In a large bowl, combine roasted Brussels sprouts, cooked quinoa, cranberries, and walnuts.
5. Drizzle with lemon juice and toss to combine. Serve warm.

Nutritional Information

Calories: 280, Protein: 8g, Carbohydrates: 40g, Fat: 10g, Fiber: 8g, Cholesterol: 0 mg, Salt: 250 mg, Potassium: 550 mg

RATATOUILLE WITH HERBED POLENTA

Servings 4 | Prep: 20 min | Cook: 40 min

This vibrant and hearty dish combines the rich flavors of ratatouille with the comforting texture of herbed polenta, making it a perfect heart-healthy vegetarian meal.

Equipment

Large Skillet, Medium Saucepan, Whisk

Ingredients

- 200 g Eggplant, diced
- 150 g Zucchini, sliced
- 150 g Red Bell Pepper, chopped
- 100 g Onion, chopped
- 2 cloves Garlic, minced
- 400 g Canned Tomatoes, crushed
- 1 tbsp Olive Oil
- 1 tsp Dried Thyme
- 1 tsp Dried Basil
- 500 ml Vegetable Broth
- 150 g Polenta
- 1 tbsp Fresh Parsley, chopped
- Salt and Pepper to taste

Directions

1. Heat olive oil in a large skillet over medium heat. Add eggplant, zucchini, red bell pepper, onion, and garlic. Sauté until vegetables are tender, about 10 minutes.
2. Stir in crushed tomatoes, thyme, and basil. Season with salt and pepper. Simmer for 20 minutes, stirring occasionally.
3. Meanwhile, in a medium saucepan, bring vegetable broth to a boil. Gradually whisk in polenta. Reduce heat to low and cook, stirring frequently, until thickened, about 10 minutes.
4. Stir in fresh parsley into the polenta. Adjust seasoning with salt and pepper.
5. Serve ratatouille over a bed of herbed polenta.

Nutritional Information

Calories: 250, Protein: 6g, Carbohydrates: 45g, Fat: 7g, Fiber: 8g, Cholesterol: 0 mg, Salt: 300 mg, Potassium: 800 mg

ASIAN-INSPIRED SESAME TOFU WITH BOK CHOY

Servings 4 | Prep: 15 min | Cook: 20 min

This dish combines the nutty flavor of sesame with the freshness of bok choy and the satisfying texture of tofu, creating a heart-healthy meal that's both delicious and nutritious.

Equipment

Non-stick skillet, Mixing bowl, Whisk

Ingredients

- 400 g firm tofu, drained and cubed
- 30 ml sesame oil
- 2 cloves garlic, minced
- 300 g bok choy, chopped
- 50 ml low-sodium soy sauce
- 10 g sesame seeds
- 5 g fresh ginger, grated
- 10 ml rice vinegar
- 5 g cornstarch mixed with 30 ml water

Directions

1. Heat 15 ml of sesame oil in a non-stick skillet over medium heat. Add tofu cubes and cook until golden brown on all sides, about 8 minutes. Remove and set aside.
2. In the same skillet, add the remaining sesame oil, garlic, and ginger. Sauté for 1 minute until fragrant.
3. Add bok choy and stir-fry for 3-4 minutes until just tender.
4. In a mixing bowl, whisk together soy sauce, rice vinegar, and cornstarch mixture. Pour over the bok choy and stir well.
5. Return the tofu to the skillet, sprinkle with sesame seeds, and toss everything together until well coated and heated through, about 2 minutes.

Nutritional Information

Calories: 220, Protein: 12g, Carbohydrates: 10g, Fat: 15g, Fiber: 3g, Cholesterol: 0 mg, Salt: 300 mg, Potassium: 450 mg

Desserts

AVOCADO CHOCOLATE MOUSSE

Servings 4 | Prep: 10 min | Cook: 0 min

Indulge in a creamy, rich chocolate mousse that's heart-healthy and guilt-free, thanks to the smoothness of ripe avocados and the depth of dark cocoa.

Equipment

Blender, Mixing Bowl, Spatula

Ingredients

- 2 ripe avocados (about 400g)
- 60g unsweetened cocoa powder
- 80ml almond milk
- 60ml honey or maple syrup
- 5ml vanilla extract
- A pinch of salt

Directions

1. Halve the avocados, remove the pits, and scoop the flesh into a blender.
2. Add the cocoa powder, almond milk, honey, vanilla extract, and salt to the blender.
3. Blend until smooth and creamy, scraping down the sides as needed.
4. Taste and adjust sweetness if necessary by adding more honey or maple syrup.
5. Spoon the mousse into serving bowls and chill in the refrigerator for at least 30 minutes before serving.

Nutritional Information

Calories: 220, Protein: 3g, Carbohydrates: 28g, Fat: 13g, Fiber: 7g, Cholesterol: 0mg, Salt: 30mg, Potassium: 550mg

OATMEAL BANANA COOKIES

Servings 12 | Prep: 10 min | Cook: 15 min

These heart-healthy oatmeal banana cookies are naturally sweetened and packed with fiber, making them a guilt-free treat that satisfies your sweet tooth while supporting heart health.

Equipment

Mixing Bowl, Baking Tray, Parchment Paper

Ingredients

- 200 g Rolled Oats
- 2 Ripe Bananas (about 200 g)
- 50 g Unsweetened Applesauce
- 50 g Chopped Walnuts
- 30 g Dark Chocolate Chips
- 5 g Ground Cinnamon
- 2 g Baking Powder
- 1 g Salt

Directions

1. Preheat your oven to 180°C (350°F) and line a baking tray with parchment paper.
2. In a mixing bowl, mash the bananas until smooth.
3. Add the rolled oats, applesauce, walnuts, chocolate chips, cinnamon, baking powder, and salt to the mashed bananas. Mix until well combined.
4. Drop spoonfuls of the mixture onto the prepared baking tray, flattening each slightly to form cookies.
5. Bake in the preheated oven for 15 minutes or until the edges are golden brown.
6. Allow the cookies to cool on the tray for a few minutes before transferring them to a wire rack to cool completely.

Nutritional Information

Calories: 95, Protein: 2g, Carbohydrates: 15g, Fat: 3g, Fiber: 2g, Cholesterol: 0 mg, Salt: 30 mg, Potassium: 120 mg

ALMOND BUTTER BROWNIES

Servings 12 | Prep: 15 min | Cook: 25 min

These Almond Butter Brownies are a heart-healthy twist on a classic dessert, offering a rich, nutty flavor with a moist and fudgy texture. Perfect for satisfying your sweet tooth without compromising your heart health.

Equipment

Mixing Bowl, Whisk, Baking Pan (20x20 cm)

Ingredients

- 200 g Almond Butter
- 100 g Dark Chocolate (70% cocoa), melted
- 150 g Unsweetened Applesauce
- 100 g Whole Wheat Flour
- 50 g Honey
- 5 g Baking Powder
- 2 g Sea Salt
- 5 ml Vanilla Extract

Directions

1. Preheat the oven to 180°C and line the baking pan with parchment paper.
2. In a mixing bowl, combine almond butter, melted dark chocolate, applesauce, honey, and vanilla extract. Whisk until smooth.
3. Add whole wheat flour, baking powder, and sea salt to the wet mixture. Stir until just combined.
4. Pour the batter into the prepared baking pan, spreading it evenly.
5. Bake for 25 minutes or until a toothpick inserted in the center comes out clean.
6. Allow to cool in the pan for 10 minutes before transferring to a wire rack to cool completely.

Nutritional Information

Calories: 210, Protein: 5g, Carbohydrates: 20g, Fat: 13g, Fiber: 3g, Cholesterol: 0 mg, Salt: 50 mg, Potassium: 180 mg

CHIA SEED BERRY PUDDING

Servings 4 | Prep: 10 min | Cook: 0 min

This delightful Chia Seed Berry Pudding is a heart-healthy dessert that combines the creamy texture of chia seeds with the natural sweetness of berries. It's a perfect guilt-free treat that is both nutritious and satisfying.

Equipment

Mixing Bowl, Whisk, Refrigerator

Ingredients

- 60 g Chia Seeds
- 500 ml Almond Milk (unsweetened)
- 100 g Fresh Mixed Berries (e.g., strawberries, blueberries, raspberries)
- 15 ml Honey or Maple Syrup (optional)
- 5 ml Vanilla Extract

Directions

1. In a mixing bowl, combine chia seeds, almond milk, honey or maple syrup (if using), and vanilla extract.
2. Whisk the mixture thoroughly to ensure the chia seeds are evenly distributed.
3. Cover the bowl and refrigerate for at least 4 hours or overnight until the pudding thickens.
4. Before serving, stir the pudding to break up any clumps.
5. Top with fresh mixed berries and enjoy chilled.

Nutritional Information

Calories: 180, Protein: 5g, Carbohydrates: 25g, Fat: 8g, Fiber: 10g, Cholesterol: 0 mg, Salt: 50 mg, Potassium: 250 mg

DARK CHOCOLATE AND WALNUT BARK

Servings 12 | Prep: 10 min | Cook: 10 min

Indulge in this heart-healthy treat that combines the rich taste of dark chocolate with the crunch of walnuts, offering a delightful balance of flavors and textures.

Equipment
Double boiler or microwave-safe bowl, Baking sheet, Parchment paper

Ingredients
- 200 g dark chocolate (70% cocoa or higher)
- 100 g walnuts, roughly chopped
- 30 g dried cranberries
- 1 g sea salt

Directions
1. Line a baking sheet with parchment paper.
2. Melt the dark chocolate using a double boiler or microwave until smooth.
3. Stir in the chopped walnuts and dried cranberries until well combined.
4. Pour the mixture onto the prepared baking sheet, spreading it evenly.
5. Sprinkle sea salt over the top.
6. Refrigerate for about 30 minutes or until set.
7. Break into pieces and serve.

Nutritional Information
Calories: 150, Protein: 2g, Carbohydrates: 12g, Fat: 10g, Fiber: 3g, Cholesterol: 0 mg, Salt: 20 mg, Potassium: 150 mg

APPLE CINNAMON BAKED OATMEAL

Servings 6 | Prep: 10 min | Cook: 35 min

This comforting Apple Cinnamon Baked Oatmeal is a heart-healthy dessert that combines the warmth of cinnamon with the natural sweetness of apples, perfect for a cozy treat.

Equipment
Baking Dish, Mixing Bowl, Whisk

Ingredients
- 200 g Rolled Oats
- 500 ml Low-Fat Milk
- 2 Apples, diced
- 50 g Honey
- 1 tsp Ground Cinnamon
- 1 tsp Baking Powder
- 1/2 tsp Salt
- 1 tsp Vanilla Extract
- 1 Egg

Directions
1. Preheat the oven to 180°C (350°F).
2. In a mixing bowl, combine oats, baking powder, cinnamon, and salt.
3. In another bowl, whisk together milk, egg, honey, and vanilla extract.
4. Pour the wet ingredients into the dry ingredients and mix well.
5. Fold in the diced apples.
6. Pour the mixture into a baking dish and bake for 35 minutes, or until golden brown.
7. Let it cool slightly before serving.

Nutritional Information
Calories: 220, Protein: 6g, Carbohydrates: 40g, Fat: 4g, Fiber: 5g, Cholesterol: 30 mg, Salt: 150 mg, Potassium: 250 mg

RASPBERRY CHIA JAM BARS

Servings 12 | Prep: 15 min | Cook: 25 min

These Raspberry Chia Jam Bars are a delightful heart-healthy treat, combining the natural sweetness of raspberries with the nutritional benefits of chia seeds. Perfect for a guilt-free dessert or snack.

Equipment

Baking Pan, Mixing Bowl, Saucepan

Ingredients

- 200 g Rolled Oats
- 150 g Almond Flour
- 60 ml Maple Syrup
- 100 g Coconut Oil, melted
- 300 g Fresh Raspberries
- 30 g Chia Seeds
- 15 ml Lemon Juice
- 5 ml Vanilla Extract

Directions

1. Preheat the oven to 180°C and line a baking pan with parchment paper.
2. In a mixing bowl, combine rolled oats, almond flour, maple syrup, and melted coconut oil. Mix until well combined.
3. Press two-thirds of the oat mixture into the prepared baking pan to form the base.
4. In a saucepan over medium heat, combine raspberries, chia seeds, and lemon juice. Cook for 5 minutes until the raspberries break down. Stir in vanilla extract.
5. Spread the raspberry chia mixture over the oat base in the baking pan.
6. Crumble the remaining oat mixture over the raspberry layer.
7. Bake for 20-25 minutes until the top is golden brown. Allow to cool before slicing into bars.

Nutritional Information

Calories: 210, Protein: 4g, Carbohydrates: 24g, Fat: 12g, Fiber: 5g, Cholesterol: 0 mg, Salt: 5 mg, Potassium: 150 mg

BLUEBERRY ALMOND CRISP

Servings 6 | Prep: 15 min | Cook: 30 min

This delightful Blueberry Almond Crisp combines the natural sweetness of blueberries with the nutty crunch of almonds, offering a heart-healthy dessert that's both satisfying and nutritious.

Equipment

Baking Dish, Mixing Bowl, Oven

Ingredients

- 500 g Fresh Blueberries
- 50 g Almond Flour
- 50 g Rolled Oats
- 30 g Sliced Almonds
- 60 ml Honey
- 30 ml Fresh Lemon Juice
- 5 g Ground Cinnamon
- 2 g Salt

Directions

1. Preheat the oven to 180°C (350°F).
2. In a mixing bowl, combine blueberries, honey, and lemon juice. Toss gently to coat the blueberries evenly.
3. Transfer the blueberry mixture to a baking dish, spreading it out evenly.
4. In the same mixing bowl, combine almond flour, rolled oats, sliced almonds, ground cinnamon, and salt. Mix well.
5. Sprinkle the almond-oat mixture evenly over the blueberries in the baking dish.
6. Bake in the preheated oven for 30 minutes, or until the topping is golden brown and the blueberries are bubbling.
7. Allow to cool slightly before serving.

Nutritional Information

Calories: 180, Protein: 4g, Carbohydrates: 28g, Fat: 7g, Fiber: 5g, Cholesterol: 0 mg, Salt: 150 mg, Potassium: 150 mg

PUMPKIN SPICE ENERGY BITES

Servings 12 | Prep: 15 min | Cook: 0 min

These Pumpkin Spice Energy Bites are a delightful, heart-healthy treat packed with the warm flavors of autumn. Perfect for a quick snack or a post-workout boost, they combine the goodness of oats, pumpkin, and spices in a convenient bite-sized form.

Equipment

Mixing Bowl, Measuring Cups, Baking Sheet (for setting)

Ingredients

- 150 g Rolled Oats
- 100 g Pumpkin Puree
- 60 g Almond Butter
- 50 g Honey
- 30 g Chia Seeds
- 1 tsp Pumpkin Spice Mix
- 1/2 tsp Vanilla Extract
- 1/4 tsp Salt

Directions

1. In a mixing bowl, combine the rolled oats, pumpkin puree, almond butter, honey, chia seeds, pumpkin spice mix, vanilla extract, and salt.
2. Stir the mixture thoroughly until all ingredients are well combined and form a sticky dough.
3. Using your hands, roll the mixture into small balls, about the size of a tablespoon each.
4. Place the energy bites on a baking sheet and refrigerate for at least 30 minutes to set.
5. Once set, store in an airtight container in the refrigerator for up to a week.

Nutritional Information

Calories: 95, Protein: 3g, Carbohydrates: 14g, Fat: 4g, Fiber: 2g, Cholesterol: 0 mg, Salt: 50 mg, Potassium: 100 mg

COCONUT AND DATE BLISS BALLS

Servings 12 | Prep: 15 min | Cook: 0 min

These delightful Coconut and Date Bliss Balls are a perfect heart-healthy treat, combining natural sweetness with a satisfying texture. They are easy to make and perfect for a quick snack or dessert.

Equipment

Food Processor, Mixing Bowl, Measuring Cups and Spoons

Ingredients

- 200 g Pitted Dates
- 100 g Unsweetened Shredded Coconut
- 50 g Almonds
- 1 tbsp Chia Seeds
- 1 tbsp Coconut Oil
- 1 tsp Vanilla Extract

Directions

1. Place the pitted dates, almonds, and chia seeds in a food processor. Blend until finely chopped.
2. Add the shredded coconut, coconut oil, and vanilla extract to the mixture. Blend until well combined and the mixture starts to stick together.
3. Transfer the mixture to a mixing bowl. Using your hands, roll the mixture into small balls, about the size of a walnut.
4. Roll each ball in additional shredded coconut to coat the outside.
5. Refrigerate the bliss balls for at least 30 minutes to firm up before serving.

Nutritional Information

Calories: 120, Protein: 2g, Carbohydrates: 15g, Fat: 6g, Fiber: 3g, Cholesterol: 0 mg, Salt: 2 mg, Potassium: 180 mg

MANGO AND COCONUT CHIA PARFAIT

Servings 4 | Prep: 10 min | Cook: 0 min

This refreshing Mango and Coconut Chia Parfait is a delightful heart-healthy dessert that combines the tropical flavors of mango and coconut with the nutritional benefits of chia seeds. It's perfect for a light and satisfying treat.

Equipment

Mixing Bowl, Whisk, Serving Glasses

Ingredients

- 400 ml Coconut Milk
- 60 g Chia Seeds
- 200 g Fresh Mango, diced
- 20 g Honey (optional)
- 10 g Unsweetened Coconut Flakes
- 5 ml Vanilla Extract

Directions

1. In a mixing bowl, whisk together the coconut milk, chia seeds, honey, and vanilla extract until well combined.
2. Cover the bowl and refrigerate for at least 2 hours or overnight, allowing the chia seeds to absorb the liquid and thicken.
3. Once set, stir the chia pudding to ensure even consistency.
4. Layer the chia pudding and diced mango in serving glasses, alternating between the two.
5. Top each parfait with a sprinkle of unsweetened coconut flakes.
6. Serve immediately or keep refrigerated until ready to enjoy.

Nutritional Information

Calories: 220, Protein: 4g, Carbohydrates: 28g, Fat: 12g, Fiber: 6g, Cholesterol: 0 mg, Salt: 10 mg, Potassium: 250 mg

CHOCOLATE-DIPPED STRAWBERRIES WITH NUTS

Servings 8 | Prep: 15 min | Cook: 5 min

Indulge in these heart-healthy chocolate-dipped strawberries, enhanced with a crunchy nut topping. Perfect for a guilt-free dessert or a romantic treat.

Equipment

Double boiler, Baking sheet, Parchment paper

Ingredients

- 200 g Dark chocolate (70% cocoa or higher)
- 500 g Fresh strawberries, washed and dried
- 50 g Mixed nuts, finely chopped (e.g., almonds, walnuts, pistachios)

Directions

1. Melt the dark chocolate in a double boiler over low heat, stirring until smooth.
2. Line a baking sheet with parchment paper.
3. Holding each strawberry by the stem, dip it into the melted chocolate, allowing any excess to drip off.
4. Roll the chocolate-coated strawberry in the chopped nuts, ensuring an even coating.
5. Place the strawberries on the prepared baking sheet and let them set in the refrigerator for about 15 minutes.

Nutritional Information

Calories: 120, Protein: 2g, Carbohydrates: 15g, Fat: 7g, Fiber: 3g, Cholesterol: 0 mg, Salt: 2 mg, Potassium: 220 mg

BAKED PEACHES WITH HONEY AND CINNAMON

Servings 4 | Prep: 10 min | Cook: 20 min

A delightful and heart-healthy dessert that combines the natural sweetness of peaches with the warm flavors of honey and cinnamon. Perfect for a light and satisfying treat.

Equipment

Baking dish, Oven, Small mixing bowl

Ingredients

- 4 ripe peaches, halved and pitted
- 30 ml honey
- 5 g ground cinnamon
- 10 g chopped almonds (optional)
- 5 ml fresh lemon juice
- 5 g unsalted butter, melted

Directions

1. Preheat the oven to 180°C (350°F).
2. Arrange the peach halves, cut side up, in a baking dish.
3. In a small mixing bowl, combine honey, cinnamon, lemon juice, and melted butter.
4. Drizzle the honey mixture over the peaches, ensuring even coverage.
5. Optionally, sprinkle chopped almonds over the peaches for added texture.
6. Bake in the preheated oven for 20 minutes, or until peaches are tender and slightly caramelized.
7. Serve warm, and enjoy the comforting flavors.

Nutritional Information

Calories: 120, Protein: 1g, Carbohydrates: 25g, Fat: 3g, Fiber: 2g, Cholesterol: 1 mg, Salt: 2 mg, Potassium: 250 mg

VEGAN PEANUT BUTTER CUPS

Servings 12 | Prep: 15 min | Cook: 10 min

Indulge in these creamy, rich vegan peanut butter cups that are both heart-healthy and deliciously satisfying. Perfect for a guilt-free dessert or snack.

Equipment

Muffin Tin, Mixing Bowl, Saucepan

Ingredients

- 200 g Dark Chocolate (70% cocoa or higher)
- 120 g Natural Peanut Butter
- 30 ml Maple Syrup
- 15 g Coconut Oil
- 1 g Sea Salt

Directions

1. Melt the dark chocolate and coconut oil together in a saucepan over low heat, stirring until smooth.
2. Line a muffin tin with paper liners and pour a small amount of the melted chocolate into each cup, just enough to cover the bottom.
3. In a mixing bowl, combine the peanut butter, maple syrup, and a pinch of sea salt until smooth.
4. Spoon a small dollop of the peanut butter mixture into the center of each chocolate-filled cup.
5. Cover the peanut butter with more melted chocolate until the cups are full.
6. Place the muffin tin in the refrigerator for about 10 minutes, or until the chocolate is set.
7. Remove from the fridge and enjoy your heart-healthy treat!

Nutritional Information

Calories: 150, Protein: 3g, Carbohydrates: 12g, Fat: 11g, Fiber: 2g, Cholesterol: 0 mg, Salt: 30 mg, Potassium: 120 mg

LEMON POPPY SEED MUFFINS

Servings 12 | Prep: 15 min | Cook: 20 min

These delightful lemon poppy seed muffins are light, fluffy, and bursting with citrus flavor, making them a perfect heart-healthy treat.

Equipment

Mixing Bowl, Muffin Tin, Whisk

Ingredients

- 200 g Whole Wheat Flour
- 50 g Poppy Seeds
- 100 g Greek Yogurt
- 80 ml Honey
- 60 ml Olive Oil
- 2 Eggs
- 1 Lemon (zest and juice)
- 5 g Baking Powder
- 2 g Baking Soda
- 2 g Salt

Directions

1. Preheat the oven to 180°C and line a muffin tin with paper liners.
2. In a mixing bowl, whisk together the flour, poppy seeds, baking powder, baking soda, and salt.
3. In another bowl, combine the Greek yogurt, honey, olive oil, eggs, lemon zest, and lemon juice.
4. Gradually add the wet ingredients to the dry ingredients, stirring until just combined.
5. Divide the batter evenly among the muffin cups.
6. Bake for 18-20 minutes or until a toothpick inserted into the center comes out clean.
7. Allow to cool in the tin for 5 minutes before transferring to a wire rack to cool completely.

Nutritional Information

Calories: 150, Protein: 4g, Carbohydrates: 20g, Fat: 6g, Fiber: 3g, Cholesterol: 30 mg, Salt: 150 mg, Potassium: 100 mg

SPICED APPLE COMPOTE WITH GREEK YOGURT

Servings 4 | Prep: 10 min | Cook: 15 min

This delightful dessert combines the natural sweetness of apples with warm spices, perfectly complemented by creamy Greek yogurt. It's a heart-healthy treat that's both satisfying and nourishing.

Equipment

Saucepan, Mixing Spoon, Measuring Cups and Spoons

Ingredients

- 500 g apples, peeled, cored, and diced
- 100 ml water
- 1 tbsp lemon juice
- 1 tsp ground cinnamon
- 1/2 tsp ground nutmeg
- 1 tbsp honey
- 400 g Greek yogurt

Directions

1. In a saucepan, combine the diced apples, water, lemon juice, cinnamon, and nutmeg.
2. Bring the mixture to a simmer over medium heat, stirring occasionally.
3. Cook for 10-15 minutes until the apples are tender and the liquid has reduced.
4. Stir in the honey and remove from heat. Allow the compote to cool slightly.
5. Serve the spiced apple compote over Greek yogurt in individual bowls.

Nutritional Information

Calories: 150, Protein: 8g, Carbohydrates: 28g, Fat: 2g, Fiber: 4g, Cholesterol: 5 mg, Salt: 40 mg, Potassium: 300 mg

BLACK BEAN AND DARK CHOCOLATE FUDGE

Servings 12 | Prep: 15 min | Cook: 20 min

This rich and decadent fudge combines the unexpected creaminess of black beans with the deep flavor of dark chocolate, creating a heart-healthy treat that's both satisfying and nutritious.

Equipment

Blender, Baking Pan, Mixing Bowl

Ingredients

- 400 g canned black beans, drained and rinsed
- 150 g dark chocolate (70% cocoa), chopped
- 100 g rolled oats
- 60 ml maple syrup
- 30 ml coconut oil, melted
- 5 ml vanilla extract
- 2 g baking powder
- 1 g salt

Directions

1. Preheat the oven to 180°C and line a baking pan with parchment paper.
2. In a blender, combine black beans, melted chocolate, oats, maple syrup, coconut oil, vanilla extract, baking powder, and salt. Blend until smooth.
3. Pour the mixture into the prepared baking pan, spreading it evenly.
4. Bake for 20 minutes or until the edges are firm and the center is set.
5. Allow to cool completely in the pan before cutting into squares.

Nutritional Information

Calories: 150, Protein: 4g, Carbohydrates: 20g, Fat: 7g, Fiber: 4g, Cholesterol: 0 mg, Salt: 50 mg, Potassium: 200 mg

CARROT CAKE ENERGY BITES

Servings 12 | Prep: 15 min | Cook: 0 min

These Carrot Cake Energy Bites are a delightful, no-bake treat that captures the essence of carrot cake in a heart-healthy form. Perfect for a quick snack or a sweet finish to a meal.

Equipment

Food Processor, Mixing Bowl, Measuring Cups

Ingredients

- 150 g Rolled Oats
- 100 g Grated Carrots
- 100 g Pitted Dates
- 50 g Almonds
- 30 g Shredded Coconut
- 30 ml Maple Syrup
- 5 g Ground Cinnamon
- 2 g Ground Nutmeg
- 2 g Vanilla Extract

Directions

1. Combine oats, almonds, and shredded coconut in a food processor. Pulse until finely ground.
2. Add grated carrots, pitted dates, maple syrup, cinnamon, nutmeg, and vanilla extract to the mixture. Process until well combined and sticky.
3. Transfer the mixture to a mixing bowl.
4. Using your hands, form the mixture into 12 small balls.
5. Place the energy bites on a tray and refrigerate for at least 30 minutes to set.

Nutritional Information

Calories: 95, Protein: 2g, Carbohydrates: 15g, Fat: 3g, Fiber: 2g, Cholesterol: 0 mg, Salt: 5 mg, Potassium: 130 mg

VANILLA CHIA PUDDING WITH BERRIES

Servings 4 | Prep: 10 min | Cook: 0 min

A delightful and creamy dessert that's both heart-healthy and satisfying. This vanilla chia pudding is topped with fresh berries, offering a burst of flavor and a boost of antioxidants.

Equipment

Mixing Bowl, Whisk, Refrigerator-safe Container

Ingredients

- 500 ml Almond Milk (unsweetened)
- 60 g Chia Seeds
- 1 tsp Vanilla Extract
- 20 g Honey or Maple Syrup
- 200 g Mixed Berries (such as strawberries, blueberries, and raspberries)

Directions

1. In a mixing bowl, whisk together the almond milk, chia seeds, vanilla extract, and honey or maple syrup until well combined.
2. Let the mixture sit for about 5 minutes, then whisk again to prevent clumping.
3. Cover the bowl and refrigerate for at least 4 hours or overnight, until the pudding thickens.
4. Before serving, stir the pudding and divide it into four servings.
5. Top each serving with a generous portion of mixed berries.

Nutritional Information

Calories: 180, Protein: 4g, Carbohydrates: 28g, Fat: 7g, Fiber: 10g, Cholesterol: 0 mg, Salt: 40 mg, Potassium: 250 mg

ROASTED PEARS WITH ALMOND BUTTER DRIZZLE

Servings 4 | Prep: 10 min | Cook: 20 min

A delightful and heart-healthy dessert, these roasted pears are tender and sweet, complemented by a rich almond butter drizzle that adds a nutty depth to each bite.

Equipment

Baking Sheet, Small Saucepan, Mixing Spoon

Ingredients

- 4 ripe pears (about 600g)
- 30 ml honey
- 15 ml lemon juice
- 60 g almond butter
- 5 g cinnamon
- 30 ml water
- 10 g sliced almonds (optional, for garnish)

Directions

1. Preheat the oven to 180°C (350°F).
2. Halve the pears and remove the cores. Place them cut side up on a baking sheet.
3. Drizzle the pears with honey and lemon juice, then sprinkle with cinnamon.
4. Roast in the oven for 20 minutes or until tender.
5. In a small saucepan, combine almond butter and water over low heat, stirring until smooth.
6. Drizzle the almond butter mixture over the roasted pears.
7. Garnish with sliced almonds, if desired, and serve warm.

Nutritional Information

Calories: 210, Protein: 3g, Carbohydrates: 35g, Fat: 8g, Fiber: 6g, Cholesterol: 0 mg, Salt: 5 mg, Potassium: 320 mg

WHOLE-WHEAT BANANA BREAD

Servings 8 | Prep: 15 min | Cook: 50 min

This heart-healthy banana bread is moist, flavorful, and packed with nutrients. It's perfect for a guilt-free dessert or a wholesome snack.

Equipment

Mixing Bowl, Whisk, Loaf Pan

Ingredients

- 240 g Whole-Wheat Flour
- 3 Ripe Bananas (about 300 g)
- 100 ml Unsweetened Applesauce
- 60 ml Honey
- 2 Large Eggs
- 5 g Baking Soda
- 2 g Salt
- 5 ml Vanilla Extract
- 50 g Chopped Walnuts (optional)

Directions

1. Preheat the oven to 175°C (350°F) and lightly grease a loaf pan.
2. In a mixing bowl, mash the bananas until smooth. Add applesauce, honey, eggs, and vanilla extract, then whisk until well combined.
3. In a separate bowl, mix whole-wheat flour, baking soda, and salt. Gradually add the dry ingredients to the wet mixture, stirring until just combined.
4. Fold in the chopped walnuts, if using.
5. Pour the batter into the prepared loaf pan and smooth the top.
6. Bake for 50 minutes or until a toothpick inserted into the center comes out clean.
7. Allow to cool in the pan for 10 minutes, then transfer to a wire rack to cool completely.

Nutritional Information

Calories: 180, Protein: 4g, Carbohydrates: 34g, Fat: 4g, Fiber: 4g, Cholesterol: 35 mg, Salt: 150 mg, Potassium: 300 mg

MATCHA GREEN TEA AND COCONUT POPSICLES

Servings 6 | Prep: 10 min | Cook: 0 min

These refreshing popsicles combine the earthy flavor of matcha with the creamy sweetness of coconut, making for a delightful heart-healthy treat.

Equipment

Blender, Popsicle molds, Measuring cups and spoons

Ingredients

- 400 ml coconut milk
- 15 g matcha green tea powder
- 60 ml honey or maple syrup
- 5 ml vanilla extract
- 30 g shredded coconut

Directions

1. In a blender, combine the coconut milk, matcha green tea powder, honey, and vanilla extract. Blend until smooth.
2. Pour the mixture into popsicle molds, leaving a little space at the top.
3. Sprinkle shredded coconut into each mold, gently stirring to distribute evenly.
4. Insert popsicle sticks and freeze for at least 4 hours or until solid.
5. To serve, run warm water over the outside of the molds to release the popsicles easily.

Nutritional Information

Calories: 120, Protein: 1g, Carbohydrates: 10g, Fat: 9g, Fiber: 1g, Cholesterol: 0 mg, Salt: 10 mg, Potassium: 150 mg

STRAWBERRY AND OAT CRUMBLE BARS

Servings 12 | Prep: 15 min | Cook: 30 min

These delightful bars combine the natural sweetness of strawberries with the wholesome goodness of oats, making them a perfect heart-healthy treat.

Equipment

Baking Dish (20x20 cm), Mixing Bowl, Saucepan

Ingredients

- 200 g Rolled Oats
- 150 g Whole Wheat Flour
- 100 g Honey
- 100 g Unsalted Butter, melted
- 300 g Fresh Strawberries, hulled and chopped
- 50 g Chia Seeds
- 1 tsp Vanilla Extract
- 1/2 tsp Ground Cinnamon

Directions

1. Preheat the oven to 180°C (350°F). Grease the baking dish lightly.
2. In a mixing bowl, combine oats, flour, and cinnamon. Stir in melted butter and honey until the mixture is crumbly.
3. Press half of the oat mixture into the bottom of the prepared baking dish to form a crust.
4. In a saucepan over medium heat, cook strawberries and chia seeds until thickened, about 5 minutes. Stir in vanilla extract.
5. Spread the strawberry mixture evenly over the crust. Top with the remaining oat mixture, pressing gently.
6. Bake for 25-30 minutes or until the top is golden brown. Allow to cool before slicing into bars.

Nutritional Information

Calories: 180, Protein: 3g, Carbohydrates: 28g, Fat: 7g, Fiber: 4g, Cholesterol: 10 mg, Salt: 5 mg, Potassium: 150 mg

SWEET POTATO CHOCOLATE CHIP COOKIES

Servings 12 | Prep: 15 min | Cook: 15 min

These cookies are a delightful blend of sweet potatoes and chocolate chips, offering a heart-healthy twist on a classic favorite. Perfectly soft and chewy, they are sure to satisfy your sweet tooth while keeping your heart in mind.

Equipment

Mixing Bowl, Baking Sheet, Parchment Paper

Ingredients

- 200 g Sweet Potato, mashed
- 100 g Whole Wheat Flour
- 50 g Rolled Oats
- 50 g Dark Chocolate Chips
- 50 ml Maple Syrup
- 30 ml Olive Oil
- 1 tsp Baking Powder
- 1 tsp Vanilla Extract
- 1/2 tsp Cinnamon
- 1/4 tsp Salt

Directions

1. Preheat the oven to 180°C (350°F) and line a baking sheet with parchment paper.
2. In a mixing bowl, combine the mashed sweet potato, maple syrup, olive oil, and vanilla extract. Mix well.
3. Add the whole wheat flour, rolled oats, baking powder, cinnamon, and salt to the wet ingredients. Stir until just combined.
4. Fold in the dark chocolate chips.
5. Drop spoonfuls of the dough onto the prepared baking sheet, spacing them evenly.
6. Bake for 12-15 minutes, or until the edges are golden brown.
7. Allow the cookies to cool on the baking sheet for a few minutes before transferring them to a wire rack to cool completely.

Nutritional Information

Calories: 120, Protein: 2g, Carbohydrates: 18g, Fat: 5g, Fiber: 2g, Cholesterol: 0 mg, Salt: 50 mg, Potassium: 150 mg

CINNAMON ROASTED ALMONDS

Servings 8 | Prep: 10 min | Cook: 15 min

These Cinnamon Roasted Almonds are a delightful, heart-healthy treat, offering a perfect balance of sweetness and spice. Enjoy them as a snack or a topping for your favorite desserts.

Equipment

Baking Sheet, Mixing Bowl, Oven

Ingredients

- 200 g Raw Almonds
- 30 ml Honey
- 10 g Ground Cinnamon
- 5 ml Vanilla Extract
- 2 g Sea Salt

Directions

1. Preheat the oven to 180°C (350°F) and line a baking sheet with parchment paper.
2. In a mixing bowl, combine honey, ground cinnamon, vanilla extract, and sea salt.
3. Add the almonds to the mixture, stirring until they are evenly coated.
4. Spread the coated almonds in a single layer on the prepared baking sheet.
5. Roast in the preheated oven for 15 minutes, stirring halfway through to ensure even roasting.
6. Allow the almonds to cool completely before serving or storing in an airtight container.

Nutritional Information

Calories: 180, Protein: 6g, Carbohydrates: 15g, Fat: 12g, Fiber: 4g, Cholesterol: 0 mg, Salt: 50 mg, Potassium: 210 mg

NO-BAKE CASHEW AND DATE BARS

Servings 12 | Prep: 15 min | Cook: 0 min

These no-bake cashew and date bars are a delightful, heart-healthy treat that combines the natural sweetness of dates with the creamy texture of cashews. Perfect for a quick snack or a guilt-free dessert.

Equipment

Food Processor, Baking Dish, Parchment Paper

Ingredients

- 200g Pitted Dates
- 150g Raw Cashews
- 50g Rolled Oats
- 30g Unsweetened Cocoa Powder
- 15ml Coconut Oil
- 5ml Vanilla Extract
- Pinch of Salt

Directions

1. Line a baking dish with parchment paper for easy removal.
2. In a food processor, combine the dates and cashews. Pulse until finely chopped.
3. Add the rolled oats, cocoa powder, coconut oil, vanilla extract, and salt. Blend until the mixture forms a sticky dough.
4. Press the mixture evenly into the prepared baking dish.
5. Refrigerate for at least 1 hour to set. Once firm, cut into bars.

Nutritional Information

Calories: 180, Protein: 4g, Carbohydrates: 24g, Fat: 9g, Fiber: 3g, Cholesterol: 0mg, Salt: 20mg, Potassium: 250mg

Printed in Dunstable, United Kingdom